Moralitis

A Cultural Virus

Robert Oulds (Bruges Group)
& Niall McCrae (King's College London)

Published in 2020 by

The Bruges Group, 246 Linen Hall, 162-168 Regent Street, London W1B 5TB
www.brugesgroup.com

Follow us on Twitter @brugesgroup, LinkedIn in @brugesgroup
Facebook f The Bruges Group, Instagram brugesgroup, YouTube brugesgroup
Bruges Group publications are not intended to represent a corporate view of European and international developments. Contributions are chosen on the basis of their intellectual rigour and their ability to open up new avenues for debate.

About the Authors

Robert Oulds MA, FRSA is the director of the Bruges Group. His master's degree is in communications management. Amongst other works, Robert is the author of *Montgomery and the First War on Terror* and *Everything You Wanted to Know About the EU But Were Afraid to Ask* (both published by Bretwalda Books), and co-author of *Federalist Thought Control: The Brussels Propaganda Machine*. Robert served as cabinet member for education in a London borough council, and as a treasurer and standard bearer for the Royal British Legion. He regularly appears on television and radio in political debate.

Niall McCrae PhD, MSc, RMN is a senior lecturer in mental health at King's College London. His previous books were *The Moon and Madness* (2011) and *Echoes from the Corridors: the Story of Nursing in British Mental Hospitals* (with Peter Nolan, 2016). Niall writes regularly for *Salisbury Review* magazine and various socio-political websites, and he campaigns for freedom of speech in universities.

Contents

Executive summary and recommendations 4

Preface 7

Part I: Cultural revolution 11

Part II: Cultural virus 37

Part III: Cultural remedy 52

Appendix A: Moralitis Questionnaire 79

Appendix B: Rebutting the Wigston Report 82

Glossary 95

References 97

Index 99

Lists of Illustrations

Diagram 1: Horseshoe 13

Antonio Gramsci (1891-1937) 16

Diagram 2: Virtue-signaling cycle 21

Diagram 3: The wokeness escalation arms race 36

Diagram 4: The stages of infection:
  symptomatic degradation of the mind, society and country 45

Executive summary and recommendations

Background

Much is written about a divided society, split between young and old, progressives and conservatives, patriots and globalists, the posh and the plebs. Perhaps it was ever thus. But there is more tension than ever, with widely diverging ways of seeing the world. As people become polarised, many fear for the future. One side worries about nationalist dictators, the other about loss of cultural security to the forces of globalisation. One side is obsessed with the rights of minorities, the other thinks that a silent majority is the dog being wagged by its tail.

In the progressive outlook, the younger, socially-liberal generations will inherit the world, and conservative nay-sayers are on the wrong side of history. Yet this perspective fails to appreciate the enduring value of faith, flag and family. Emancipatory activism has brought significant improvements to the rights and social inclusion of previously disadvantaged groups, but it did not stop at equality, and the demands of identity politics have become more aggressive, if not absurd.

Enlightenment values of freedom of speech, democracy and equality before the law are being eroded by censorship and moral relativism. The euphemism 'political correctness' has taken a more extreme form, with young social justice warriors identifying themselves as 'woke'. With the political and cultural establishment behind them, their ideas have been elevated to the status of moral hegemony. Contrary opinion is quashed, and ordinary people are afraid to speak their minds.

Moralitis

In this treatise we argue that society is infected with a cultural virus. Moralitis is a disorder of the mind, spread throughout society by ideological pathogens. Symptoms of this delusional syndrome include rejection of common sense and conventional social norms, uncritical acceptance of subversive ideology, inflexibility of thought, cultural self-loathing and reflex denunciation of dissent. The afflicted may think that they act with autonomy but they are progressively controlled by the virus. Parroting group-think, they virtue-signal at every opportunity, and police moral compliance in conversations and on social media. The moralitic make life a misery for themselves and others.

Prevention and treatment

While some believe that we are nearing a turning point, the cultural sickness is so pervasive that it will get much worse before it gets better. Antibodies exist in the form of contrarians who courageously speak out against stifling conformity and irrational ideas, but they lack critical mass. The woke have been radicalised, and it would be futile to attempt to cure their illness with reason alone. Therefore, a concerted effort is needed, akin to a public health strategy, to eradicate moralitis. Our main recommendations are shown below.

Recommendations

We propose a radical programme of general and specifically-targeted interventions:–

1. End 'cancel culture': appoint free speech advocates and introduce mandatory training in civil liberties in all organisations (public, private and voluntary sectors) with a workforce of 70+

2. Promotion of 'plainspeak': Orwellian language to be banished from public documents

3. A virtue-signalling 'swear box' to be installed in every workplace

4. School reform: introduction of specific learning opportunities to engage in different opinions, to develop respect and resilience; headteachers to be legally bound to meet parents on any concerns about ideologically-motivated changes to curricula (e.g. transgender propaganda)

5. Establish an inspectorate for universities, taking a carrot-and-stick approach: awards for promoting debate and creative endeavor, and penalties for censorship or political discrimination

6. Impact assessments on any government or local authority policy that could undermine national / local identity

7. Repeal the Equality Act and hate crime legislation, replacing these with a Statute of Liberty; reinstate the Statute in Restraint of Appeals and terminate judiciability of the European Court of Human Rights

8. Stop funding hate: no more public money to groups that exacerbate division in society

9. A rigorous enquiry into the anti-Christian, anti-conservative and anti-patriotic bias in the BBC, with the withdrawal of the television licence

10. Identity politics to be banished from the armed services, and rejection of the Wigston Report into 'inappropriate behaviours'

11. Root-and-branch reform of the Civil Service to the will of the people as expressed in elections, through better recruitment and promotion processes; appoint a Wokefinder General in Whitehall, reporting to the Cabinet

12. A Royal Commission of Enquiry to be appointed with a broad remit to investigate the impact of subversive ideology on society

Alongside such institutional reforms the theme of liberty should be emphasised at every turn. Hearts and minds will be won by promoting the very freedoms denied by the moral puritans who govern our lives. Just as dehumanizing fascism and communism were defeated, so too will wokeness.

Preface

The advanced societies of the future will not be governed by reason. They will be driven by irrationality, by competing systems of psychopathology.

JG Ballard[1]

Society is infected. Like the growth of bacteria in a Petri dish, subversive postmodern ideology has spread through the collective mind. The march through the institutions, as urged by Italian communist Antonio Gramsci, is almost complete. Replacing the social class struggle of the nineteenth and twentieth centuries is the pursuit of identity politics, rationalised by moral relativism and policed by 'political correctness'.

From transubstantiation to transgenderism

In the religious piety of past centuries, it was dangerous to doubt Roman Catholic creed. It was blasphemous, for example, to suggest that the Eucharist is merely symbolic, and not literally the body and blood of Christ. Today, forced belief and inquisition is focused on sexual politics, with the new doctrine of transgenderism. First puberty blockers then gender-bending hormones are given to children who were influenced by messages from gender-confused peers about being born in the wrong body[2] [3] [4]. Binary sex is rejected: men can menstruate and women can have testes. The laws of nature are redefined as social construct, and any dissent causes furore. How has such unscientific and irrational ideology taken hold on society?

As the Jesuits and Lenin understood, minds are most malleable at the earliest age. Fundamental beliefs about society are internalised by a process of individual

---

1   Ballard JG (2003): Letter. https://www.researchpubs.com/products-page-2/j-g-ballard-quotes-autographed-lexibind-softbound-editions-excerpts-on-the-future/

2   British Psychological Society (17 January 2018): Most children and teens with gender dysphoria also have multiple other psychological issues. https://digest.bps.org.uk/2018/01/17/most-children-and-teens-with-gender-dysphoria-also-have-multiple-other-psychological-issues/

3   BBC News (15 October 2019): Questions remain over puberty-blockers, as review clears study. https://www.bbc.co.uk/news/health-50046579

4   LifeSite (5 September 2018): Study: Teen gender confusion associated with 'trans' peer groups, prior mental health issues. https://www.lifesitenews.com/news/study-teen-gender-confusion-associated-with-trans-peer-groups-prior-mental

attunement to a collective ethos. Each new generation has tended to create its own identity and outlook, tending to challenge the world view of elders. The youth of today, though, is pushing the agenda further; like in the Cultural Revolution of Chairman Mao, parents are denounced for being too moderate. As philosopher John Gray[5] stated, 'progressivism has become the unthinking faith of millions of graduates'. They call themselves 'woke', and the future, according to teenage prophet Greta Thunberg[6], belongs to them.

A world of wokeness

National identity is a casualty of this progressive morality. Like Trotsky's mission of international socialism, the European Union undermines the nation state and traditional social bonds. Demarcation by gender, sexual orientation and ethnicity is central to its policy-making and funding, and bodies representing special interest groups are expected to promote pan-Europeanism. Federalist propaganda has been highly effective. Anti-Brexit rallies following the EU referendum warned that minority groups would be deprived of their rights. Who would have thought, after the Second World War, that multitudes of younger people would march through London waving the flag of a continental regime, believing their own country to be incapable of governing itself and protecting its own citizens?

Indeed, the progressive values of the establishment and brainwashed younger people have become hegemonic. Family breakdown, 'helicopter parenting' and a feminised education system in which feelings trump fact have contributed to the young accepting moral absolutes as a comfort blanket protecting them from the burden of responsibility. Masculinity, no longer a virtue, is regarded as toxic; 'soyboys'[7] apologise for being male. Open borders are an ethical essential; patriotism is bigotry. Immersed in postmodern ideology, compliant millennials are distracted from the real problems in society such as wage stagnation and rising costs of living, uncontrolled immigration and seismic cultural change.

After the resounding victory by Boris Johnson in the 2019 general election, is

---

5   Gray J (2020): The new battleground. *New Statesman.* 17-13 January: 22-26.
6   Thunberg G (2019): *No One is Too Small to Make a Difference.* London: Penguin.
7   'Slang used to describe males who completely and utterly lack all necessary masculine qualities. This pathetic state is usually achieved by an over-indulgence of emasculating products and/or ideologies.' *Urban Dictionary. https://www.urbandictionary.com/define.php?term=Soy%20Boy*

the tide turning? Wokeness is becoming *passé*, according to a *Times* columnist[8]. But this would be complacent. Postmodern philosophy is deeply engrained in our culture and its institutions. Ostensibly, the emphasis on equality and diversity simply teaches us to be nice to others, but the underlying purpose is control. As witnessed with the refusal of the metropolitan elite to accept the result of the EU referendum, power and privilege are not readily relinquished. Despite being of an electoral majority, few Conservative or Brexit supporters dare to speak up in a politically hostile environment. The electorally vanquished will regroup, and try to reinforce their cultural authority.

Army dreamers

Civil servants, teachers, human resources departments and policymakers have become indistinguishable from social justice warriors, obsessed with imaginary defects in their organisational culture. Appended to this monograph is our report on the subversive ideological onslaught in the armed services, where the 'top brass' is burnishing its progressive credentials. The new government has a chance to undo the damage of the postmodern era, but will it tackle the divisive and damaging ideology that prevents competent administration and true leadership? Otherwise, we will have only woke soldiers to defend us.

A cultural virus

In this monograph we present our thesis of a cultural sickness, a delusional syndrome that drives people to reject common sense and conventional social norms. We have isolated a specific pathogen. Moralitis has cytopathic effect on society, controlling cognition and behaviour. Among its most aggressive symptoms is reflex denunciation of anyone as 'deeply offensive' for expressing the wrong opinion or using the wrong word. Racism, sexism and 'transphobia' are everywhere! The afflicted may seem to act with autonomy, but the forces of conformity are such that their freedom is limited, and their utterances merely regurgitations of group-think.

The moralitic do not perceive anything wrong with themselves, because the symptoms are an expression of apparently positive ideals (tolerance, equality and diversity). Whereas an infection such as influenza impairs physical fitness, this

---

8   James Marriott (17 December 2019): The woke revolution is burning itself out. *Times.* https://www. thetimes.co.uk/article/the-woke-revolution-is-burning-itself-out-scxmz7djp

cultural virus enhances social fitness. While many older people have developed resistance, the young are more susceptible due to their lack of immunity gained from 'real world' experience. The disease propagates on social media, where moral hubris frequently erupts in hysteria. The germ cannot reproduce on its own, but infiltrates brain cells, using the host to communicate the virus in social settings. In the worst cases of neurodegeneration, prion cells mutate in such a way that all reason is lost.

As the rate of infection has reached pandemic level, an antidote is urgently needed. Moralitis has done enough damage, and must not be allowed to fester. In this work we present a treatment plan to eradicate the virus from society. Indeed, we hope that this book is a vaccine in itself.

Part I: Cultural revolution

They appeared to be relatively harmless, nutty-professor refugees with funny foreign accents who were seeking shelter in America, pleading tolerance for lofty ideals.
Michael Walsh[9]

Left and Right: as they were

The political dichotomy of 'left' and 'right' originally appeared in the French revolution of 1789, when members of the national assembly divided into supporters of the king to the president's right and revolutionary supporters to his left. Broadly, the Left is socially progressive and economically controlling, while the Right is economically liberal and socially conservative, as differentiated by Nick Watt[10], chief political correspondent for the *Guardian*:–

'At its most basic level I would use leftwing to describe a party that believes the state can play a benign, though not necessarily a dominant, role in the governance of society. I would use rightwing to describe a party that is wary of state intervention and believes in lower taxes as a way of stimulating economic growth and giving people greater freedom.'

Stable democracies such as Britain have oscillated between governments of moderate Left and Right[11], having a fairly even distribution of followers on each side, with elections decided by a relatively small number of 'swing voters'. Sometimes the shift is large enough to produce a landslide, as achieved by Tony Blair's 'New Labour' in 1997. By definition, extremists do not appeal to the majority, and fail to prosper in polls. While younger people are more inclined to vote for socialist or egalitarian parties, older people are drawn to the

---

9   Walsh M (2015): *The Devil's Pleasure Palace: the Cult of Critical Theory and the Subversion of the West*. New York: Encounter.

10   *Guardian* (9 March 2015): Political labels are useful — but only in moderation. Quoted in article by Chis Elliot. https://www.theguardian.com/commentisfree/2015/mar/09/political-labels-useful-only-in-moderation-greens-ukip

11   We use Left and Right as proper nouns, hence with capitals. However, in adjective form (e.g. left-leaning, right-wing), lower case is used.

conservative side of the spectrum. This is attributed to the optimistic idealism of youth and the pessimistic realism of the old. Yet the cause may be that the young are drawn to absolutes, especially ideas that can be enacted by authoritarian systems. Mature generations know that most things political come in shades of grey, rather than black or white.

The dichotomy of progressive versus conservative is often applied judgmentally. For example, in the EU referendum the BBC characterised Remain voters as open and Leavers as closed. Authoritarianism, the inclination to control other people, is often positioned on the Right and liberalism on the Left, but this is an erroneous idea influenced by political bias in academe. Although the leftist student activism of the 1960s was libertarian, campaigns for freedom of speech increasingly involve people pejoratively labelled as right-wing.

Authoritarianism is a personality trait, varying from high to low in the populace. A pioneer in its study was Hans Eysenck[12] at the Institute of Psychiatry at The Maudsley Hospital. Influenced by his childhood experience in Nazi Germany and from meeting British communists, Eysenck's seminal observation was that people with highly authoritarian personalities are attracted to dictatorial politics whether of the Left or Right. Thus fascists readily switch to communism (or *vice versa*) should one regime replace another. However, the far-Right tends to be regarded as more dangerous than the far-Left. The Conservative administration under Theresa May highlighted right-wing extremism as a similar threat to that of Islamist terror. The hard Left is presumed as politically legitimate, despite the violence of groups such as Antifa.

Personality researcher Adam Perkins[13] argued that government efforts to tackle extremism would fail if the political ideology is targeted, because those with authoritarian personality traits will shift to another political outlet. Instead, Perkins argued, democracy should be promoted, as this starves extremists of power. However, radical parties have sometimes won elections in national crisis, and moved swiftly to consolidate their position by suppressing democratic process.

Eysenck's theory of authoritarian personality traits has been reinforced by recent

---

12   Eysenck HJ (1954): *The Psychology of Politics*. London: Routledge & Kegan Paul.
13   Perkins A (30 November 2015): Authoritarianism is a matter of personality, not politics. *Quillette*. https://quillette.com/2015/11/30/authoritarianism-is-a-matter-of-personality-not-politics/

research[14] [15]. The confluence of Left and Right at the political extremes was depicted by French political scientist Jean-Pierre Faye[16] as a horseshoe, with the sides converging at the ends.

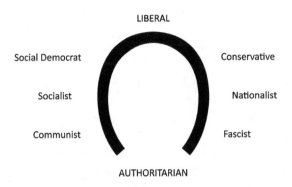

Diagram 1: Horseshoe

Some on the Left are offended by the horseshoe, arguing that their side is benevolent while the Right is discriminatory. However, in the words of George Orwell[17] socialists have a 'hypertrophied sense of order', and it is this trait that links the extremes of Left and Right. They both like laws, and lots of them. The horseshoe makes sense of regimes that display aspects of Left and Right. The Nazi party in Germany is regarded as purely right-wing although it literally began as national socialism. The original Italian fascism was a state ideology that sought to resolve and eliminate class conflict through a corporatist system of governance; it was a development of Marx's dictatorship of the proletariat. The Spanish Falangismo movement, of which General Franco became leader, was overtly anti-capitalist. China remains communist but is increasingly orientated to Han nationalism. Both Left and Right become more collectivist and utilitarian in their farther reaches. Free-thinkers are not welcome in a means-to-an-end polity.

14   De Regt S, Mortelsman D, Smits T (2011): Left-wing authoritarianism is not a myth, but a worrisome reality: evidence from 13 Eastern European countries. *Communist & Post-Communist Countries*, 44: 299-308.

15   Ludeke SG, Krueger RF (2013): Authoritarianism as a personality trait: evidence from a longitudinal behaviour genetic study. *Personality & Individual Differences*, 55: 480-484.

16   Faye JP (1996): *Le Siècle des Idéologies*. Paris: Arman Colin.

17   Orwell G (1937/2001): *The Road to Wigan Pier*. London: Penguin Classics.

Psychologist Jonathan Haidt[18] compared six moral concerns across the political divide:–

1. Care versus harm	4. Loyalty versus betrayal
2. Liberty versus oppression	5. Authority versus subversion
3. Fairness versus cheating	6. Sanctity versus degradation

Left-leaning respondents regarded the first three concerns as highly important, but had little interest in the other three. Primarily concerned with equality and diversity, they were wary of patriotism and religion. Right-wing respondents valued all concerns equally. Understanding of fairness differed between the two groups: those on the Right measured this by opportunity, left-wingers by outcome. Haidt conducted a further survey, asking respondents of Left and Right to rate the moral concerns as if they were on the opposite side. While the right-wing group predicted rival responses accurately, left-wing respondents believed that the Right is not interested in care, liberty or fairness.

Meanings of Left and Right are shaped by whichever side gains cultural supremacy. The younger graduate generations, influenced by a progressive education system, are reinforcing a predominantly liberal-left establishment. The Right is often fantasised in extreme form by both the liberal mainstream as callous capitalism and jingoistic xenophobia, and a staging-post to 1930s-style fascism. Left is virtue; Right is vice.

Cultural Marxism

Postmodern ideology derives from cultural Marxism. This is a contentious term, often wrongly associated with grand conspiracy theories exciting the liberal-Left[19]. Literally, cultural Marxism refers to the shift in focus from the economic determinism of Karl Marx to social mores[20]. Communist and socialist states had shown the difficulties of manipulating human motivation and behaviour. As efforts to eradicate faith, folklore and family loyalty floundered, Marxists realised that nothing changes unless the underlying culture is changed. Guidance for this

---

18   Haidt J (2012): *The Righteous Mind: Why Good People are Divided by Politics and Religion*. Penguin.
19   McCrae N (10 October 2018): Cultural Marxists don't like being called Cultural Marxists. *Bruges Group*. https://www.brugesgroup.com/blog/cultural-marxists-don-t-like-being-called-cultural-marxists
20   Kurten D, McCrae N (16 September 2019): The problem with cultural Marxism. *European Conservative*. https://europeanconservative.com/2019/09/the-problem-with-cultural-marxism/

reorientation came from the critical theorists of the Frankfurt School, including Max Horkheimer, Theodor Adorno and Herbert Marcuse. As many of the founders were Jews who fled from Nazi persecution in the 1930s, the concept of cultural Marxism is often criticised as an anti-Semitic trope. However, these men were Marxists, pursuing an ideology at odds with Judaism[21] [22] [23].

The Frankfurt School professors were aware that the labouring masses in the democratic West would not agitate for a Soviet-style communist revolution like the Bolsheviks in 1917. Although these people had hard lives, conditions were slowly improving due to capitalist economics tempered by Christian philanthropy, trade union representation and an expanding franchise. They were too patriotic to follow 'pied pipers' who threatened to bring the whole house down. Against this prevailing preference for continuity over change, critical theory initiated a relentless assault on the foundational elements of our culture that maintain stability, order and belonging. An important difference between economic and cultural Marxism is that rather than promoting mass revolt, the postmodern project divides people into distinct groups with distinct demands.

From his itinerant chair in American academe, Herbert Marcuse combined Freudian ideas with Marxism in *Eros and Civilisation*, his premise being that Western civilisation, with its Judeao-Christian mores, was inherently repressive[24]. Although stopping short of the orgasmic obsession of his contemporary Wilhelm Reich (whose orgone accumulator was parodied in Woody Allen's film *Sleeper*), the thinking was basically the same. Marcuse termed society 'monogamic-patriarchal', postulating that freedom depended on the West escaping from its ritual prison to become 'polymorphous-perverse'. Encouraging sexual anarchy, Marcuse coined the phrase 'make love, not war', the slogan of the 1960s sexual revolution.

In Britain, where the main vehicle for cultural Marxism was the New Left project, Antonio Gramsci is better known than Marcuse. Jailed for communist agitation

---

21   Newman S (25 October 2006): Are we all Cultural Marxists now? *Conservative Home*. https://www.conservativehome.com/platform/2006/10/dr_simon_newman.html

22   Indeed, some of these nominally Jewish figures wanted to destroy religion, a point made by Rabbi Marvin S Antelman (1974): *To Eliminate the Opiate*. Zahavia.

23   Melanie Phillips(11 November 2009):We were fools to think the fall of the Berlin Wall had killed off the far Left. They're back — and attacking us from within. *Daily Mail*. https://www.dailymail.co.uk/debate/article-1226211/MELANIE-PHILLIPS-We-fools-think-fall-Berlin-Wall-killed-far-Left-Theyre--attacking-within.html

24   Murphy PA (26 April 2014): Antonio Gramsci: take over the institutions! *American Thinker*.

in Italy, Gramsci mused in his *Prison Notebooks* on why social stratification had persisted in the West, and suggested how to create the revolutionary conditions to pave the way for socialism. Civic society was strong in the countries of western Europe, but could be weakened by a Marxist onslaught, aiming beyond the 'economic substructure' to the 'cultural superstructure'. This would be a slow process, in the phrase coined by radical German student leader Rudi Dutschke: 'a long march through the institutions'. By stealth, cultural Marxists have pushed the boundaries, often meeting little resistance.

Antonio Gramsci (1891-1937)

One might ask how and why the theories of obscurantist left-wing intellectuals should prevail long after their deaths. Few among the younger generations have heard of Marcuse. The answer is that cultural Marxism, while rarely known as such, is a potent strategy for dismantling society and diluting its traditions. While it would be absurd to describe the elites of the political establishment, commerce, the media and banking as Marxists, their pursuit of power has similar revolutionary principles and practices. Promoting minorities while disabling the majority creates a divided populace that is more readily controlled. Unelected transnational bodies destroy the democratic nation-state from above, while the undemocratic influence of mega-financier George Soros[25] and his Open Society Foundation hollows out nations from within. The old dictum of divide and rule has come to the fore in the cultural Marxist schema of identity politics.

Identity politics

The term 'progressive' is used without a clear idea of destiny: where is this progress leading? Like the Frankfurt School, the postmodern philosophers of the Parisian Left Bank[26] strove to break the stable rock of society. Deconstructionist Jacques Derrida, Michel Foucault with his 'everything is power' cynicism and psychobabbler Jacques Lacan were building on shifting sand, but they did not intend to settle there. Discrimination, a rallying cry to be used against the system, was a concept in constant flux. From the 1960s onwards, people of particular race, ethnicity, gender or sexual orientation organised themselves politically to assert their rights. This kaleidoscope of emancipatory movements may have changed society for the better, but apparently equality is not enough. The ethical stance of identity politics is moral relativism; in George Orwell's words, 'some are more equal than others'[27].

Defined by their ethnic or sexual status, people are represented collectively regardless of whether they like such identification or the views expressed on their behalf. Ironically, while biological essentialism has been eschewed for social constructionism, identity constructs are applied in an essentialist way. Female gender, black ethnicity and homosexuality are conferred with absolute value in terms of vulnerability and victimhood; protected status gives immunity from criticism, and anyone who quibbles with this is perceived as morally suspect. For example, a balanced consideration of domestic violence is almost impossible, just as gay marriage was no longer open to debate when legalised. Most women, people of black and Asian ethnicities, and gay men and lesbians, do not expect or demand special treatment, but the voices of militants are heard over the sensible majority.

Social value is based on a simplistic demarcation of oppressors and oppressed.

25   *Independent* (28 May 2019): What is the Bilderberg Group and are its members really plotting the New World Order? https://www.independent.co.uk/news/world/europe/bilderberg-group-conspiracy-theories-secret-societies-new-world-order-alex-jones-a8377171.html

26   Sarup M (1993): *An Introductory Guide to Post-Structuralism and Postmodernism.* Hemel Hempstead: Harvester Wheatsheaf.

27   Orwell G (1945/1987): *Animal Farm.* London: Penguin.

Before stepping out of the house in the morning, men are generalised as the patriarchy, white people are guilty of racism, 'straight' women reinforce heteronormative bias, and Christians need not pray in public to discriminate against gay people or Muslims. However, a person could have good and bad identities: a white atheist lesbian is noble in all but her colour. Least favoured in the intersectionality[28] of identity politics is the white heterosexual male (a charge to which both authors plead guilty).

Electorally, there is great potential in appealing to a 'rainbow alliance' of identity groups. Advocating this approach was the feminist pamphlet *Beyond the Fragments*[29], which arose from the authors' frustration with macho left-wing politics; they sought to empower marginalised groups without relegating their status as secondary to broader class struggle. However, sorting of society by gender, ethnicity and other criteria has been criticised as divisive. Former Archbishop of Canterbury Rowan Williams argued that identity politics and claims for minority rights are causing fragmentation of society; instead we should focus on the common good[30]. Celebration of other ethnicities is promoted to the neglect of the host culture. As argued by Trevor Phillips[31], former head of the Equality & Human Rights Commission, a cohesive society cannot be built on separate communities. Meanwhile the poor performance of white working-class boys in the education system is ignored by middle-class administrators, who fail to help children simply because they belong to two proscribed identity groups[32].

Identity politics activism has learned from the targeted tactics of the marketing industry. Segments of society are idealised, and members of the chosen group are encouraged directly or subliminally to be the person portrayed by advertisements (e.g. the 'perfect mum'). Such images may be artificial, but by constant

---

28 Intersectionality was conceived by feminist Kimberlé Crenshaw to highlight additional discrimination against black women. It has since morphed into a grand theory of structural inequity in society. Coleman Hughes (14 January 2020): Reflections on intersectionality. *Quillette*. https://quillette.com/2020/01/14/reflections-on-intersectionality/

29 Rowbotham S, Segal L, Wainwright H (1979): *Beyond the Fragments.*

30 *Daily Telegraph* (27 March 2012): Rowan Williams: fixation with gay rights, race and feminism threatens society. https://www.telegraph.co.uk/news/religion/9169536/Rowan-Williams-fixation-with-gay-rights-race-and-feminism-threatens-society.html

31 *Guardian* (16 March 2015): Trevor Phillips says the unsayable about race and multiculturalism. Article by Michael White. https://www.theguardian.com/uk-news/2015/mar/16/trevor-phillips-race-multiculturalism-blog

32 *Daily Telegraph* (16 November 2018): Boys left to fail at school because attempts to help them earn wrath of feminists, says ex-Ucas chief. https://www.telegraph.co.uk/education/2018/11/16/boys-left-fail-school-attempts-help-earn-wrath-feminists-says/

reinforcement the marketing man's myth becomes real. Politicians jumped on this bandwagon, and by the 1990s election campaigns created symbolic groups (e.g. 'Mondeo man'[33]). People are fixed into discrete communities and encouraged to accentuate their difference. Like commercial marketing, political targeting of identity groups encourages a sense of need. However, this differs from the aspiration promoted by advertisers; the message of identity politics is social justice, as defined by progressive ideology.

From material to moral currency

In his book *Affluenza*, psychologist Oliver James[34] railed against consumerism and how people are driven to compete by displaying wealth through luxury goods and leisure. However, in liberal capitalist economies with a moderately redistributive taxation system, cars, holidays, electronic gadgets and other symbols of wealth are no longer the preserve of the rich. As the affluent middle class cannot easily distinguish itself materially, it has turned to moral value to mark its superiority over the uncultured lower strata. Consequently, we argue that 'affluenza' now manifests in a class-bound moral competitiveness.

Whereas in the past our morality was guided by religious scruples, the modern landscape is secularist. Indeed, as faith declines in Western culture (though not in the growing Islamic populace), the state is replacing not only God but also the family. Consider the ideological fervour by which the NHS is defended, and also middle-class enthusiasm for a universal salary, whereby every adult would receive a standard guaranteed income from the state (putatively, a monetary realisation of egalitarian virtue). Indeed, the religiosity of a state is inversely proportional to the strength of its welfare system[35]. There is no better attack on conservativism or the 'Protestant work ethic' than the elevation of the state to an all-encompassing provider. Family breakdown is rife, while the dyad of 'stay-at-home mother' and breadwinner husband is disparaged. Encouraged to work, mothers are publicly funded to leave their children from the youngest age to nurseries, where their moral education can begin.

Moral rectitude is displayed by virtue signalling. Mostly this is a public

---

33   The Ford Mondeo was a common company car.
34   James O (2007): *Affluenza*. Vermilion.
35   Gruneau Brulin J, Hill PC, Laurin K, Mikulincer M, Granqvist P (2018): Religion vs. the welfare state—the importance of cultural context for religious schematicity and priming. *Psychology of Religion & Spirituality*, 10: 276–287.

performance so routine and ritualistic that the person who is speaking or posting an online message is merely adhering to norms. A minority, however, seeks and exploits opportunities to display their values, repeating mantras in a quasi-religious piety. There are social, occupational and material rewards for public displays of virtue, and individuals and institutions play the game. A blatant example is the Young Vic Theatre in London, where four flags are hung on the façade: the gay rainbow, transgenderism, the EU and 'Black Lives Matter'. The intended message is: 'look how progressive we are', with a corollary of sticking two fingers up at any socially conservative patriots who happen to pass by.

The internet is a shop window of moral currency. If you apply for a job, it is highly likely that an employer will survey your social media profile. In the Soviet Union a worker's advancement was not based on merit, but on their approval as a good communist. It was a system built on nomenclature. In East Germany people had two personas: the public reflection of the party line, and the private being, although the Stasi inserted listening bugs wherever it suspected dissent. A 'social credit' scheme has been introduced in China, whereby each person is scored by an algorithm measuring the desirability of his or her social media interaction[36]. Instead of liberating people, the internet has become a powerful tool for authoritarian states, but thought control is increasingly applied in the supposedly liberal West. A casual joke or careless remark on social media can rapidly lead to a person being ostracised. Postmodernists have overturned the old order only to create a new puritanism[37].

---

36   *Independent* (10 April 2018): China ranks citizens with a social credit system – here's what you can do wrong and how you can be punished. https://www.independent.co.uk/life-style/gadgets-and-tech/china-social-credit-system-punishments-rewards-explained-a8297486.html

37   Ridley M (4 February 2017): A new puritanism explains why some feminists are making common cause with Islam. *Spectator Life.* https://blogs.spectator.co.uk/2017/02/9751112/

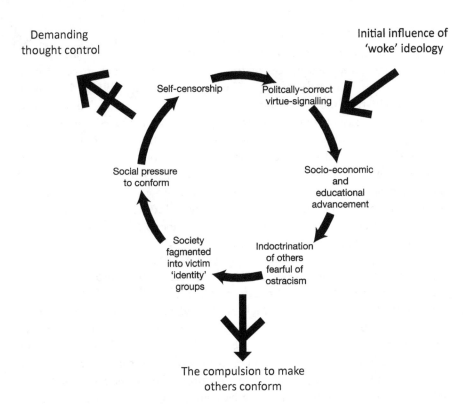

Diagram 2: Virtue-signaling cycle

Inversion of party politics

In a smoke-filled working men's club, a trade unionist puts himself forward as prospective parliamentary candidate for the Labour Party. He has worked in the colliery for twenty years, and as shop steward fought for better conditions for his colleagues. Between chain-smoking and glugs of ale, a heavy dialect emphasises his status as 'one of us'. That was the labour movement in decades past. Today, this former mining constituency has an all-female shortlist, and the favoured candidate has come up from London for a safe seat. This middle-class politics graduate sees much to improve in the town, not least the backward attitudes of some in the community. They should learn to welcome their new neighbours from abroad, standing with them against the nasty Tories. Local people may be concerned about immigration, Brexit and job insecurity, but the Labour representative wants to focus on food banks, universal credit and diversity.

Instead of the Left versus Right of previous decades, the political fault line is between the progressive morality of the metropolitan middle class and the faith, flag and family allegiances of the ordinary people (encompassing both the workers of 'old Labour' and Conservative-voting 'middle England'). David Goodhart named these respectively as 'Anywheres' and 'Somewheres'. Amounting to roughly a quarter of the population, 'Anywheres' dominate our culture and institutions, including universities and the professions. Relatively wealthy, they live in urban, multicultural areas and enjoy travelling abroad. They consider themselves sophisticated, which one dictionary defines as 'deprived of native or original simplicity'[38]. 'Somewheres' are more numerous (half of the population) and are rooted in place (which may include settled communities of black or Asian ethnicity, who generally vote for Labour). They may not be rich financially, but have strong social assets.

'Anywheres' have always been politically engaged and disproportionately influential, but recent elections have worried them. Middle-class Remainers were shocked by the EU referendum result: many had not met any Leavers in their workplaces, among their friends or on social media. On radio and television they came across Nigel Farage, who plays the role of pantomime villain in the liberal imagination, but mostly they heard the unequivocal views of the metropolitan bubble. From Remainers' perspective, an ill-informed multitude was lured to the polling stations by 'populism', a pejorative concept that is difficult to distinguish from democratic popularity. As the 'will of the people' was defied for over three years by the political establishment and judiciary[39], a frequent argument in the likes of the *Guardian* was that such a crude plebiscite endangered democracy. This recalls the old adage that if voting changed anything it would be banned.

Brexit revealed a remarkable inversion of politics. While the traditional working-class base was sceptical towards the EU, urban areas produced an overwhelming vote for Remain. Overall most Labour parliamentary seats voted Leave, and this created a major dilemma for the party. The historic alliance of the workers and Fabian intellectuals was falling apart. In the 2017 general election, when Canterbury was won by Labour for the first time in history; this was initially attributed to the high student population, but the changing voting pattern was also apparent in the presence of Labour placards in posh streets and their

---

38   Merriam-Webster *Dictionary.* www.merriam-webster.com/dictionary/sophistcated
39   Saunders R (2019): Democracy distorted. *New Statesman.* 20 December — 9 January: 32-37.

absence in the council estates[40]. Meanwhile, the deprived former coalmining town of Mansfield elected a Conservative MP.

This shift in political demography began decades ago, after the collapse of communism in eastern Europe and the decline of heavy industry and loss of faith in socialist solutions in the West. The economic (moderated Marxist) centralised planning of the Left had proved counter-productive. Like the Poujadistes, the 1950s French political movement that opposed an overbearing state, the ordinary people prefer social tradition to socialism. The mission of liberal-left parties today is no longer socialist, but the advance of multiculturalism, feminism and LGBTQ+ rights. They claim to be fighting for equality, but really this is a self–serving middle-class campaign undermining traditional society.

Current feminism is more concerned with the gender pay gap in overpaid BBC presenters than the breadline income of cleaners. There is much money to be made in discovering new ways in which women are discriminated against. The book *Invisible Women* by Carole Criado Perez[41], for example, finds sexism everywhere. According to this analysis, women are dying from a 'gender health gap', despite the clearly evident life gap in their favour, with men having an average shortfall of four years and significantly lower health service use. But it's the narrative that counts. The middle-class Women's Equality Party was launched at a time when girls outperform boys in education, and young women earn more than men of the same age. The notion of male privilege is also at odds with the homelessness gap, victims of violence gap, the prisoner gap, the suicide gap and child custody gap. And the notion of white privilege is preposterous to the lower social classes in 'left behind' towns. Labour stopped listening to the downtrodden, preferring the new radicalism of identity politics.

The traditional labour movement became an anachronism to the 'Brahmin Left'[42]. Instead of being lauded as the bedrock of society, the working class has disappointed the Labour Party. Not surprisingly, core supporters have lost faith in politicians who no longer respect them. A similar phenomenon can be seen in the USA, where the working-class vote has switched to the Republicans.

---

40   Claridge A (2018): A middle class betrayal. *Salisbury Review*, summer: 18-19.
41   Criado Perez C (2019): *Invisible Women: Exposing Data Bias in a World Designed for Men.* Chatto & Windus.
42   The Brahmins are the elite of the Indian social caste hierarchy (Brahma is the supreme being of the Hindu pantheon).

Tom Frank[43] described this trend back in 2004 in the book *What's the Matter with Kansas*, a title epitomising the arrogance of the political establishment: it's the voter's fault. But these voters are reacting to perceived snobbery and condescension of middle-class Democrats towards them. Terms such as 'flyover states', 'white trash' and Hillary Clinton's infamous 'basket of deplorables' slur hardly endear seaboard liberals to ordinary Americans.

As the old division of Left and Right weakens, Western society has become more polarised than ever[44]. According to political scientists Roger Eatwell and Matthew Goodwin[45] this dealignment has fired a surge in populism. Contrary, however, to this thesis, the populism derided by liberal globalists is neither a new phenomenon nor did it arise from the right. No major political movement has identified itself as populist since the People's Party, a left-wing agrarian movement that aimed to reform the Democrat Party in the nineteenth century. It is a term used to discredit and delegitimise those who resist the cultural and demographic revolution being foisted upon them. Social revolutionaries smear patriots to silence and disenfranchise them.

The determination of the political establishment to prevent Brexit was aided by a three-quarters majority of MPs in the House of Commons for Remain, including almost all of the Labour parliamentary party (despite most its seats having voted Leave). Rod Liddle[46] urged a reformation of political parties in Britain:–

> 'An enormous proportion of the country is in effect disenfranchised. These are the people who live outside London and dislike identity politics, political correctness and untrammelled immigration, who support Brexit and feel rooted in their community and nation, and are proud of both. But they are also poorly paid and resent the growing divide between north and south and between rich and poor. Who can they vote for?'

43   Frank T (2004): *What's the Matter with Kansas: How Conservatism Won the Heart of America*. New York: Metropolitan.

44   McCrae N (16 June 2019): The divided state of Britain. *Human Events*. https://humanevents. com/2019/06/16/the-divided-state-we-are-in/

45   Eatwell R, Goodwin M (2018): *National Populism: the Revolt against Liberal Democracy*. London: Penguin.

46   Liddle R (16 December 2018). So three people of no particular gender, nationality or religion walk into a bar. *Sunday Times*. https://www.thetimes.co.uk/article/so-three-people-of-no-particular-gender-nationality-or-religion-walk-into-a-bar-ftbhfqt9c

In the 2019 general election the 'Red Wall' of Labour northern seats crumbled, as voters preferred the 'Get Brexit done' pledge of Boris Johnson to the offer of a second EU referendum by Remain-dominated Labour. Government minister Michael Gove boasted that for the first time, both the Notting Hill Carnival and Durham Miners' Gala will be held in Conservative constituencies[47]. Northerners reacted to their vote to leave the EU being ignored, and being smeared as stupid and racist into the bargain.

So Goodhart's social divide has been verified at the ballot box. Brexit and the demise of the traditional Labour vote show that economic security is not as important as cultural security. The working class is not interested in identity politics and sanctimonious notions of 'white privilege', 'toxic masculinity' and ninety-nine genders. 'Anywheres' may have assumed moral supremacy, but 'Somewheres' retain their common-sense reality.

Boris Johnson, however, is not Donald Trump. Like a bull in a china shop, the American president is a discontinuity of socially liberal revolution returning it to the *status quo ante*. By contrast, Boris Johnson has already shown a tendency for continuity. A liberal at heart, he leads a party stuffed with parliamentarians who are conservative in name only. It is the Conservative government that has introduced transgender teaching in schools, and gender-fluid toilets have been installed on its watch. Many Conservative MPs opposed Brexit (although the worst offenders were expelled before the election) and many are as keen as those on the opposition benches to signal their progressive virtue. So perhaps it is not inversion of politics, but convergence[48]. When voters realise that both parties are as bad as each other, perhaps Britain too will get a Trumpian overhaul. Brexit was merely a beginning.

East and West swap places

Older eastern Europeans know much about Marxism, having had this totalitarian ideology imposed on them. The Soviet occupation severed people from their traditional bonds and national identities, supported by appeasers and ideologues in the West .Wilhelm Reich was among many Western intellectuals

---

47 Although this was not quite true. *News Chronicle* (13 December 2019): Michael Gove gloats that Durham Miners' Gala will now take place in a Tory seat — but he's wrong. https://www.chroniclelive.co.uk/news/north-east-news/michael-gove-gloats-durham-miners-17414323

48 For more on convergence see Tucker Carlson (2018): *Ship of Fools; How a Selfish Ruling Class is Bringing America to the Brink of Revolution*. New York: Free Press.

who saw communism as the future and welcomed the Kremlin policy of cultural eugenics. Soviet Marxists strove to create a new consciousness whereby people would relinquish old tie of faith and family to evolve into universal, identity-free workers. Cultural Marxists, by contrast, are moulding people into universal identity-free consumers. Whereas the socialists of the twentieth century hoped for a more productive and materially richer worker, the woke elites now nurture cheap labour from a mass of mobile Morlocks[49], at the whim of their enlightened social superiors.

State socialism failed both economically and politically in eastern Europe and in the USSR, which ceased to exist. The attempt to wipe the slate clean of peasant culture and the mysticism of holy Russia failed. The leukocytes resisted the invasive germ of Marxism in the body politic. Nations of eastern Europe have undergone remission, and the imposition of Soviet communism has inoculated those states against cultural Marxism. The white blood cells have strengthened immunity. The family is the focus of government welfare programmes in Hungary[50]. Poland, while welcoming more than a million from neighbouring Ukraine, rejected the European Union's attempts to offload a multitude of primarily Muslim migrants. Chancellor Merkel's reckless opening of the border and using the EU to force a quota on other European states was seen as both an affront to national sovereignty and a threat to Christian civilisation. Indeed, Christian culture has been strengthened by the efforts of Marxists and neoliberals to obliterate it.

In western Europe, however, the people were naïve to the ravages of Marxism, and have not developed resistance to the totalitarian subversion of traditional society. Like the 'new man' of Soviet planning, the EU is trying to create the postmodern European person. The main political battle being fought is not over the role of the nation-state in the lives of its citizens, but a question of whether there is any viable sovereignty and democratic polity in the context of federalism. The shift of power from national parliaments to supranational institutions has enabled a self-serving technocratic elite to evolve from being a 'class in itself' to a 'class for itself'[51]. Patriots are the underdog against globalists, but a revolt has

---

49   In HG Wells' dystopia *The Time Machine* (1895), the beautiful people (Eloi) were served by the underground Morlocks, who provided their food and clothes and tended their machinery.

50   Melanie McDonagh (30 January 2020): Buda baby boomers. *Standpoint*. https://standpointmag. co.uk/issues/february-2020/buda-baby-boomers/

51   Shore C (2003): European Union and the politics of culture. *Bruges Group*. https://www.brugesgroup. com/media-centre/papers/8-papers/900-european-union-and-the-politics-of-culture

been brewing for many years. As the riots by *gilets jaunes* in France indicate[52], government neglect is stoking the ire of the masses. 'Extremists' are setting fire to cars and vandalising speed cameras. The *Guardian* describes them as right-wing; the *Telegraph* suspects leftists. The protestors don't care how they are labelled. They have lost faith in politicians and their media lackeys.

The elephant in the room

Everyone can see the elephant in the room, but they pretend that it isn't there. Criticism of the level or impact of mass immigration has become too inflammatory for public discourse, despite the sheer scale of arrivals from abroad and the dramatic cultural change. Nonetheless, it is socially rewarding to speak of the benefits brought by incomers, or of broader ideals of multiculturalism and open borders. Attitudes to immigration are simplistically dichotomised into welcoming all or raising the drawbridge. In reality, ordinary people do not think like this, but the liberal-left establishment controls the debate.

Fifty years ago Enoch Powell delivered his infamous diatribe against immigration policy. After the Second World War, Britain tapped into its colonies in the West Indies, Africa and Asia to fill gaps in the workforce. Immigrant communities were concentrated in grim concrete housing projects inspired by le Corbusier's socialist vision of communal living. These flats were eschewed by the native population who had been forced out of their terraced homes under slum clearance programmes, and eventually moved out to the suburbs or beyond. More immigration was encouraged to fill the space in these Brutalist developments[53]. The 'sink estate' emerged as, contrary to the hopes of the central planners, residents were atomised in these decks in the sky, and physical and moral decay took hold.

As a Wolverhampton MP, Powell was sensitive to the concerns of poorer constituents about the surging influx. His prophecy of racial strife became known as the 'Rivers of Blood' speech. Immediately sacked by Ted Heath from the Conservative shadow cabinet, Powell was supported by many in the white working class, as demonstrated by a march by London dockers[54]. Known as 'tribune of the people', his speech influenced tighter controls applied by the Immigration Act 1971.

---

52   *Gilets jaunes* are named after the yellow vests that motorists are required to carry in the boot of their cars. The protests began when fuel tax was increased.
53   BBC (2012): *The Secret History of Our Streets*. https://www.bbc.co.uk/programmes/b04bzppg
54   Sandbrook D (2006): *White Heat: a History of Britain in the Swinging Sixties*. London: Abacus.

The 'Rivers of Blood' oratory has been marked in mainstream media as a turning point in race relations. There is no race war. Mixed-heritage couples and their offspring have shattered simplistic racial distinctions. The overtly racist National Front was never widely supported, and a British sense of fairness and backing the underdog was as evident as prejudice (for example, the 1967 film *To Sir with Love*, in which Sidney Poitier played a West Indian teacher in a tough East End school, was very popular). Today we have a mayor of London of Pakistani Muslim background, and a chancellor of the exchequer and home secretary of Indian ancestry. Five decades after Powell's speech, there is widespread acceptance that Britain is represented by multiple ethnicities.

Until the end of the twentieth century, immigration was carefully managed, allowing a small annual inflow on specified entry criteria. Governments were wary of worrying the electorate. This changed after the election of 'New Labour' in 1997, when the floodgates were opened. Since then, millions have arrived from Africa and Asia, and millions more from eastern Europe under EU freedom of movement rules. The ethos of integration was replaced by a multiculturalist approach that preserves distinct cultural identities and practices. On a wave of popularity, Blair swept aside any critics. As one of his aides remarked, multiculturalism was a means of 'rubbing their noses in diversity'[55]. Lord Mandelson, grandson of socialist planner Herbert Morrison, admitted to 'sending out search parties for immigrants'[56].

The establishment tends to portray a liberal immigration policy as wholly advantageous. Economically, the labour influx is a remedy for an ageing population. It is often said that the NHS would fall apart without its legions of foreign staff, although this overlooks the demand on health services of a net influx of half a million people, particularly as most incomers are net recipients of the state purse. In 2009 it was calculated that a foreign person was registering with a doctor's surgery in England and Wales every minute[57]; according to

---

55 *Daily Telegraph* (23 October 2009): Labour wanted mass immigration to make UK more multicultural, says former adviser. https://www.telegraph.co.uk/news/uknews/law-and-order/6418456/Labour-wanted-mass-immigration-to-make-UK-more-multicultural-says-former-adviser.html

56 *Daily Telegraph* (14 May 2013): Labour 'sent out search parties for immigrants', Lord Mandelson admits. https://www.telegraph.co.uk/news/uknews/immigration/10055613/Labour-sent-out-search-parties-for-immigrants-Lord-Mandelson-admits.html

57 *Daily Telegraph* (28 December 2009): Migrants joined GP practices every minute. *https://www.telegraph.co.uk/news/uknews/immigration/6858412/Migrants-joined-GP-practices-every-minute.html*

government statistics, 6.5 million immigrants registered with general practices in a ten-year period to 2017.

According to Ben Broadbent, deputy governor of the Bank of England, low-skilled immigration has contributed to a stalling in wage growth at the lower levels of the job market. The EU's system of social dumping has led to a reliance of cheap labour and retarded the need to invest in tooling and technology, thus lowering UK productivity[58]. As a 'double-whammy' on working people, mass immigration makes it harder to get a well-paid job and inflates rent and living costs. GDP has increased in paper but the share of the pie for those on lower incomes has shrunk. The affluent have benefitted from the oversupply of labour, which has depreciated the value of manual or low-skilled labour. This is not just right-wing reaction: according to ardent Labour-supporting *Guardian* columnist Polly Toynbee, 'immigration is now making the rich richer and the poor poorer'[59].

Indeed, the stratum of society most affected by uncontrolled immigration is the working class, which suffers most from overwhelmed public services, lowering wages and housing shortage. 'Somewheres' balk at the sudden and irreversible change to their towns and cities, which are becoming unrecognisable. Sometimes this provokes the white working class into voting for anti-immigration parties, but generally Labour has taken votes for granted in these areas. However, in recent elections Labour has been punished for wanting to open the doors wider to the outside world.

There is consolation for Labour in working class rejection of its progressive prospectus, in that this segment of the population is shrinking. Demography is destiny. According to the UK Statistics Authority, over a third of children born in Britain in 2016 had at least one foreign parent; in London it was two-thirds, and in Newham almost nine in ten. The UK, like other Western European nations, will soon have an electorate that is less than half indigenous, as does London already. The Muslim population has risen steadily, due to inflow and

---

58   *Guardian* (23 September 2015): UK wage growth stifled by tepid investment and low-skilled migration. https://www.theguardian.com/business/2015/sep/23/uk-wage-growth-stifled-by-tepid-investment-and-low-skilled-migration

59   Toynbee P (11 August 2006): Immigration is now making the rich richer and the poor poorer. *Guardian*. https://www.theguardian.com/commentisfree/2006/aug/11/comment.politics

larger families, by conservative estimate reaching 13 million by 2050[60].

Large voting *blocs* are nurtured by Labour, ultimately replacing one set of voters with another. Having co-opted minority groups that are socially disadvantaged and thus deserving of special treatment, the middle-class Left has created a comfortable position for itself, benefiting from cheaper goods and services of immigrant labour, while displaying virtues of tolerance and social justice. They have moralised free movement, demonising those who want to protect the livelihood of their family and community. Immigration thus brings material and moral currency. Its promotion as 'cultural enrichment' suggests something wrong with the host culture. This tendency to deprecate one's own countrymen is a manifestation of class snobbery towards the lower orders.

Critics of immigration are caricatured by the metropolitan middle class as 'white van man', a burly bloke with tattoos, who reads the *Sun* newspaper but hasn't opened a book since school. During a by-election campaign in Rochester, shadow minister and Islington MP Emily Thornberry (also known by her title of Lady Nugee) posted an image on Twitter of a house sporting a St George's flag, with a van in the driveway. She denied ridiculing the resident's patriotism, but few believed her[61]. The liberal elite associates expressions of national pride with xenophobia, and Brexit is regarded as a foretaste of fascism. After the 2019 general election, former BBC presenter Paul Mason[62] concluded that this was 'a victory of the old over the young, racists over people of colour'.

As singer Morrissey[63] remarked, 'racism' has become the most meaningless word in the English language. It is uttered by condescending latter-day missionaries who present themselves as saviours of minority groups from the native *oiks*. Yet their quaint view of people of other ethnicities derives from a paternalistic form of racism. By conferring a perpetual victim status on the immigrant, they overlook the ability of children of recent arrivals to prosper in the education

---

60   *Daily Telegraph* (29 November 2017): Muslim population of the UK could triple to 13m following 'record' influx. https://www.telegraph.co.uk/news/2017/11/29/muslim-population-uk-could-triple-13m-following-record-influx/

61   *Guardian* (23 November 2014): Emily Thornberry 'damaged Labour's election prospects with Rochester tweet'. https://www.theguardian.com/politics/2014/nov/23/emily-thornberry-damaged-labour-election-prospects-rochester-tweet

62   Paul Mason (13 December 2019): Post on Twitter. https://twitter.com/paulmasonnews/status/1205247632135872516?lang=en

63   *NME* (6 June 2018): Morrissey elaborates on support of For Britain party, says treatment of EDL founder Tommy Robinson is 'shocking'.

system and economically thereafter.

Affluent liberals gain social credit from talking about diversity, but their flight log suggests a preference for white European culture. They have the means to emigrate to rustic havens in Italy or France, far from the madding crowd. Self-declared virtuosity diverts attention from their privileged position in life, but scratch the surface and their own racism, normally projected on to others, appears. For example, on the BBC *Politics Live* discussion show, MP Angela Smith[64], who defected from Labour to join the pro-EU Change UK party, referred to black and minority ethnic people of being 'funny... ' She may have meant their colour, or perhaps cultural practices, but her internal censor quickly terminated the sentence before more damage was done. Smith later apologised for her *faux pas*.

The supposedly enlightened attitude to immigration is ironic given the escalating concern about human ecological damage. As Alp Mehmet of Migration Watch explained, immigration and higher birth rates among recent-arrival communities are driving relentless population growth. The official solution to the resulting housing problem is not to control demand but to increase supply. Millions more homes are to be built, but with no end in sight, we'll soon need millions more. Precious green space and agricultural land is lost; Portakabins are erected over school playgrounds; blocks of flats proliferate on the skyline and reach ever higher. As *Guardian* writer Oliver Burkeman[65] observed, 'every new human is a new consumer with their own footprint'. Yet open-border enthusiasts cannot answer when they are asked for an upper limit.

To avoid accusations of racism, some commentators try to confine debate to numbers, arguing that an annual influx of hundreds of thousands is unsustainable. But just as important is the cultural change. Perceiving a liberal immigration policy as inherently progressive is absurd on considering the very conservative cultures being imported. Indeed, civil liberties could be threatened by the growth of fundamentalist Islam, with its regressive mores and cultural practices that deny equality of the sexes and freedom of speech and belief. Hard-

---

64   *BBC News* (18 February 2019): Former Labour MP Angela Smith criticised over skin colour comment. https://www.bbc.co.uk/news/av/world-47283899/former-labour-mp-angela-smith-criticised-over-skin-colour-comment

65   Although the Guardian would never suggest that migrant communities stop procreating. Oliver Burkeman (13 February 2010): Climate change: calling planet birth. *Guardian.* https://www.theguardian.com/environment/2010/feb/13/climate-change-family-size-babies

won liberties are more likely to be restricted by fundamentalist religious creeds that the secularist liberal-left would lambast were it a sudden and surprising Christian revival. The European Court of Human Rights has ruled that besmirching the reputation of Prophet Mohammed is not protected by freedom of speech.[66] According to Tommy Möller[67], professor of political science at Stockholm University, Swedish society is disintegrating due to unprecedented immigration and cultural segregation:–

> 'The social putty that makes a democratic welfare society of our kind possible risks being torn apart'.

A previously safe society, Sweden is now plagued by bombings in its cities, although the government denies any link to immigration[68]. Perhaps by the time that liberals realise their mistake, it will be too late[69]. As Eric Kaufmann[70] suggested, with its multiculturalist agenda, liberal society sows the seed of its own destruction. A *Salisbury Review* writer prophesied:–

> 'The decadent culture of the declining West, fixated on the rights of 'the other', will be replaced by a vigorous manly culture which can replicate itself. Isn't history the account of the rise and fall of civilisations?'[71]

Free speech as hate speech

The concept of hate speech originated in the 1980s in the USA, where activists became frustrated by the First Amendment, which ensures freedom of speech. After several court judgments in favour of controversial speakers, legal professors created a category of speech that would be exempt from constitutional rights.

66 Tim Stanley (27 October 2018): European courts risk corroding free speech to create special status for Islam. *Daily Telegraph*. https://www.telegraph.co.uk/news/2018/10/27/european-courts-risk-corroding-free-speech-create-special-status/

67 *Breitbart* (8 January 2020): Professor: Sweden's society may be 'dissolving' due to mass migration. https://www.breitbart.com/europe/2020/01/02/professor-sweden-society-dissolving-due-to-mass-migration/

68 *Breitbart* (15 January 2020): Swedish politician says govt has lost control after huge Stockholm bombing. https://www.breitbart.com/europe/2020/01/15/swedish-politician-says-govt-has-lost-control-after-huge-stockholm-bombing/

69 *Sun* (4 January 2020): Muslim population of England smashes three million mark for first time ever, figures reveal. https://www.thesun.co.uk/news/10669341/muslim-population-england-smashes-three-million-mark-for-first-time/

70 Kaufmann E (2010): *Shall the Religious Inherit the Earth? Demography and Politics in the Twenty-First Century*. Profile.

71 Miller A (2018): The great replacement. *Salisbury Review*.

Although hate speech was never established as a legal entity, it was institutionalised by the American establishment as a means of censorship. Free speech is now regarded on campuses and in liberal-left media as a right-wing menace.

In the UK there is no specific law against hate crime, but various statutes can be used to prosecute actual or perceived comments about people of protected status. The following definition of hate crime was agreed by the Crown Prosecution Service and police forces[72]:–

> 'Any criminal offence which is perceived by the victim or any other person, to be motivated by hostility or prejudice based on a person's race or perceived race; religion or perceived religion; sexual orientation or perceived sexual orientation; disability or perceived disability and any crime motivated by hostility or prejudice against a person who is transgender or perceived to be transgender.'

No evidence is needed for a report of hate speech to be recorded by police. Harry Miller, a former police officer, was pursued by Humberside Police after posting criticisms of a proposed legal reform to gender identification on Twitter[73]. Miller was visited at work by PC Mansoor Gul, who said: 'I'm here to check your thinking'. Miller was told that although he had not committed any crime, his tweets had been recorded as a 'non-crime hate incident' under College of Policing guidelines. Gul told Miller: 'You have to understand, sometimes in the womb, a female brain gets confused and pushes out the wrong parts, and that is what transgender is'. When Miller queried this, PC Gul replied: 'I've been on a course'.

From Miller's perspective, this police action had a 'chilling effect' on his right to free speech. The High Court in London ruled that Miller's expression was lawful, and that police had acted disproportionately. The judge likened the police action to the Gestapo. However, Miller failed in his broader challenge to police pursuit and recording of hate incidents. The judge ruled that College of Policing guidance is compliant with Article 10 of the European Convention of

---

72 Metropolitan Police (accessed 28 January 2020): What is hate crime? https://www.met.police.uk/advice/advice-and-information/hco/hate-crime/what-is-hate-crime/

73 *Daily Telegraph* (14 February 2020: Police compared to Stasi and Gestapo by judge as he rules they interfered in freedom of speech by investigating 'non crime' trans tweet. https://www.telegraph.co.uk/news/2020/02/14/police-compared-stasi-gestapo-judge-rules-interfered-freedom/

ights. In response. the College of Policing[74] said: 'we want everyone to
:o express opinions as passionately as they wish without breaking the
this is preposterous. Miller broke no law yet he was harassed by police.
The BBC reported Miller's case by leading with the claim of the transgender
lobby that it was now 'open season' for transphobia, but if anything is open
season it is the abuse of police powers against members of the public who have
merely expressed an opinion.

Supposedly liberal democracies have become obsessed with policing speech.
Perpetrators of hate crime are vilified in mainstream and social media, and will
struggle to get a job. In the totalitarian regimes of China and the USSR, thought
criminals were treated more harshly than recidivists: a professor guilty of dissent
found himself below a murderer in the prison camp hierarchy. We seem to
be going the same way in the West, where liberal judges are lenient to brutal
thugs and armed burglars while jailing people for expressing their political views
against the establishment. Commenting on immigration, for example, could
easily be reported as hate, and the Old Bill will be knocking on your door.

Postmodernism not for dummies

The cultural revolution that began in the 1960s was driven by an expanding
middle class. As described by a *New Statesman* writer[75], an educated generation
gained critical mass and confronted the conservative establishment:–

> 'This new middle class long ago broke with the patrimony of its parents'
> generation and exchanged conservatism for social liberalism. It was a
> product of the growing public sector professions and the expanding
> modes of communication concentrated in the cities. Its class power
> was derived from its control over institutions of culture, media and
> learning, and its function as the national arbiter and communicator of
> aesthetic taste and values. It produced a liberal intelligentsia that was
> cosmopolitan, individualistic and, on the whole, anti-establishment.'

But then the postmodernists became the establishment. A classless society was
declared, although the meritocracy that replaced it was laden with unchecked

---

74   *Times* (15 February 2020): Judge warns police over 'Orwellian hate crimes'. https://www.thetimes.
     .uk/article/dont-behave-like-gestapo-over-transphobic-tweets-warns-judge-zc9fpw3k8
     athan Rutherford (2019): From Woodstock to Brexit: the tragedy of the liberal middle class. *New*
     sman, 20 December — 9 January: 44-49.

privilege, and a self-serving elite reinforced its status. Progressive ideolo⟨ hardly challenged. When historian Francis Fukuyama[76] announced 'the ⟨_ of history' following the collapse of communism and earlier defeat of fascism and Nazism, he believed that social liberalism had won. An advanced stage of human development had been reached. But this hubristic notion did not take long to be proved wrong, when two airliners were flown into the twin towers of the World Trade Centre in New York.

Middle-class hegemony has begun to crack. This is primarily caused not by external forces of far-right bogeymen and Islamist terror, but by its own extremism. The conflicting demands of identity politics cannot be contained indefinitely. The paradox of postmodernism was illustrated by Muslim parents in Birmingham protesting about gender teaching in primary schools[77]; cognitive dissonance was shown on the face of local MP Jess Phillips, as two favoured minority groups were at loggerheads instead of being united against the white capitalist patriarchy bogeymen. Increasingly the middle-class elite is making a fool of itself. For example, Richard Leafe, head of the national parks authority for the Lake District exclaimed that the lakes are too white, and that muddy paths deter black and minority ethnic communities from visiting. He probably expected praise but drew howls of derision. Privileged virtue-signallers have become a tiresome spectacle[78].

The advance of competing interests under the banner of identity politics is adding to the complexity of multiple and often contradictory truths which people are expected to follow. As the ratchet tightens, only the most educated and sophisticated can navigate their way through the intricate social rules that require the renunciation of common sense. This extreme etiquette is seemingly beyond the comprehension of the lower classes from which the woke wish to differentiate themselves. As explained in a scathing critique by left-wing scientist Alan Sokal, postmodernism is damaging the very social justice causes that it was supposed to help, because it is has abandoned reality in favour of an emotive and irrational phenomenology of grievance. How, then, can truth be spoken to

---

76   Fukuyama F (1992): *The End of History and the Last Man.* New York: Free Press.
77   Melanie McDonough (19 October 2019): Should Muslim parents be allowed to challenge LGBT lessons? *Spectator.* https://www.spectator.co.uk/2019/10/should-muslim-parents-be-allowed-to-challenge-lgbt-lessons/
78   Phillips T (31 December 2019). *Daily Mail.*

power?[79] The intelligentsia has fallen into a delusional state, lacking insight. We need to understand the problem before we can fix it.

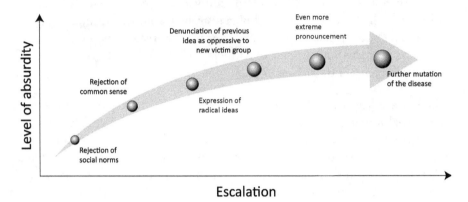

Diagram 3: The wokeness escalation arms race

79   Sokal A (2008): *Beyond the Hoax: Science, Philosophy and Culture*. Oxford: Oxford University Press.

Part II: Cultural virus

It is the folly of too many, to mistake the echo of a London coffee-house
for the voice of the kingdom.

Jonathan Swift[80]

Transmission of culture

Culture is a socialisation process. According to social learning theorist Albert Bandura[81], children instinctively imitate role models and peers without need for encouragement and reward. In the dual inheritance theory of Luca Cavilla-Sforza and Marcus Feldman, evolution has two strands: cultural and biological[82]. As in Charles Darwin's original theory[83], culture evolves through a process of variation, competition and inheritance, but is transmitted through learning (nurture) rather than by genes (nature)[84]. Cultural evolution was considered by Darwin in *The Descent of Man*[85], and the idea was developed by geneticist Richard Dawkins[86].

In *The Selfish Gene*, Dawkins argued that human beings are mere conduits for the survival of genes. He introduced the term 'meme' for a unit of cultural transmission (e.g. ideas, fashion) equivalent to a gene and following the same rule of natural selection. This concept has not been verified scientifically but has heuristic value in our understanding of cultural continuity and change. The meaning of meme has broadened to include 'an image, video, or set of text that becomes popular and spreads rapidly via the internet'[87]. The digital era has generated a much wider social learning environment with rapidly changing norms. Traditionally, enculturation primarily involves parents, family

80   Swift J (1711): *The Conduct of the Allies.*
81   Bandura A (1975): *Social Learning & Personality Development.* New Jersey: Holt, Rinehart & Winston.
82   Cavilla-Sforza LL, Feldman MW (1981): *Cultural Transmission and Evolution.* Princeton: Princeton University Press.
83   Darwin C (1859/1968): *The Origin of Species.* London: Penguin.
84   Boyd R, Richeson P (1985): *Culture and the Evolutionary Process.* Chicago: University of Chicago Press.
85   Darwin C (1871/2003): *The Descent of Man.* London: Gibson Square.
86   Dawkins R (1976): *The Selfish Gene.* Oxford: Oxford University Press.
87   *Urban Dictionary* (2017): Meme. www.urbandictionary.com/define.php?term=meme

and friends, teachers and peers, but cyberspace has expanded the number and diversity of 'cultural parents'.

Memes have been likened to germs in communicable disease, being spread by social interaction. A rapidly growing meme is described as 'going viral'. The epidemiological model of memetics is criticised for its negative connotations, as it pathologises beliefs and denies autonomy. This raises the sociological tension between structure and agency: human beings are unique individuals, yet they are governed by collective interests and social norms. The success of the marketing industry demonstrates that people can be influenced directly or subtly by unsolicited messages. Ideas are more likely to be uncritically accepted if they are prevalent in the person's social environment, as in campus culture.

Experiments in the 1950s by Solomon Asch[88] confirmed the powerful influence of the majority: participants knowingly chose a false answer to a question if everybody else gave that answer. Memes do not need factual validity to reach far and wide. The Islamic tradition of *isnād* entails a chain of transmission of the words and deeds of Mohammed, as written in *hadiths* and *sunnah*; veracity of truth depends not on evidence but on the authority of the teller. Memes may be latent for many years before proliferating. For example, the idea of cultural appropriation began in obscure Californian academic literature decades ago, but it suddenly proliferated in the present, more receptive environment. This means the inappropriate use of minority cultural expression by members of the dominant majority. The cultural appropriation meme has now taken hold, as in restrictions on fancy — dress parties, prohibition of the African 'corn row' hairstyle in white schoolchildren, and frowning on People of white European ancestry practicing yoga[89]. Rather than a positive process of multicultural cross-fertilisation this meme reinforces the oppressed / oppressor narrative. Take care at Hallowe'en parties.

Moralitis

Subversive ideology has spread so rapidly and widely, and with such profound impact, to be considered as a cultural virus. We have named this 'moralitis'. To be sure, we mean not a corporeal disease of the brain, but a psychosocial malady

---

88   Asch SE (1956): Studies of independence and conformity (I): a minority of one against a unanimous majority. *Psychological Monographs:General & Applied*, 70: 1-70.

89   McCrae N (30 October 2017): Hallowe'en and humour under attack. *Conservative Woman*. www. conservativewoman.co.uk/niall-mccrae-halloween-humour-attack

of the mind. Symptoms of moralitis include corrupted rationalism, infantile reasoning, inflexibility of thought and expression, language constraint, cultural self-loathing and a reflexive intolerance of conflicting beliefs ('ideallergy'). Simplistic polarising of people and ideas as good or bad reveal a symptomatic degradation of the mind. Moralitis prevents younger people from maturing to the ability to engage in debate or to see any faults in their ideological absolutism.

Organisational hypochondria by proxy and corporate dysmorphic disorder leads to managers anxiously obsessing over moral awareness and compliance in the workplace. Moralitis is concentrated in metropolitan areas of affluence and in towns and cities with high student populations, and throughout our political and cultural institutions. People who contract the virus may be divided into two types. First are the carriers. Not active propagators, they learn what to say and what values to convey. As a large brigade of foot-soldiers, they maintain compliance among peers through social pressure and shunning of offenders. Conformity is key to their passage in life.

The second type is the contagious. This is the forthright minority, enthused by cultural Marxism, who police social discourse and whose activism advances the cause. Often it is such people who are promoted to positions of power. Superspreaders sweep others along in their moral crusade. They are most likely to be found in the following places:–

- Critical social sciences (women's studies, media studies, black studies)

- Student unions

- Campaigners for minority / social justice causes

- Momentum (hardline activist group within the Labour Party)

- Teacher training institutes and teaching unions

- The arts

- Marketing industry

- The Duke and Duchess of Sussex

For the moralitic, truth is something to manage, rather than to understand. Ideally, beliefs should be based on facts, but for cultural Marxists facts are based on beliefs. As this causes cognitive dissonance, various mechanisms protect the believer from reality. An Orwellian dictum is that 'he who controls the language controls the debate'[90]. Many words are banned, as in the vocabulary of 'Newspeak' in Orwell's *Nineteen Eighty-Four*[91], which shrinks rather than expands over time. Topics that the prevailing culture finds uncomfortable are given euphemistic, generalised labels, such as 'Asian grooming gangs' for the widespread and organised rape of white schoolgirls by men of Pakistani Muslim background[92]. Neologisms, meanwhile, are devised for people expressing conservative views, such as 'transphobic', 'cis-gendered' and 'Islamophobic'[93]. The word 'woke' is itself an example of this crytolect[94], a language created to confuse outsiders and to differentiate the enlightened from the lower orders.

Whereas activists in the 1960s were fervently anti-establishment, the target is now the ordinary people, who are reluctant to accept the progressive agenda. Noam Chomsky described 'a herd of independent minds marching in support of state power'[95]. Supposedly liberal Western governments are stifling freedom of speech using laws against 'hate speech'. Arguably, this Kafkaesque concept not only protects minority groups but exploits identity politics to exert draconian powers over the populace. A daily average of nine persons are arrested by British police for 'improper use of public electronic communications network' under the Communications Act 2003, section 127[96]: 'black Marias' at dawn, merely for expressing a politically — incorrect opinion on Twitter or Facebook. So, while the values of the dominant culture are cloaked in liberal philosophy, progressive polity is highly authoritarian. Diversity of belief is quashed, with the support of moralitis-infected younger people who have been persuaded that words are

---

90 A dictum attributed to various writers.

91 Orwell G (1949/1989): *Nineteen Eighty-Four*. Harmondsworth: Penguin.

92 McCrae N, Harradine K (3 June 2018): Muslim rape gangs and the inconvenient truth. *Rebel Priest*. https://www.julesgomes.com/single-post/Muslim-rape-gangs-and-the-inconvenient-truth

93 Discrimination against Muslims as people is wrong, but criticism of a religion must be allowed in a free society. The term 'Islamophobia' was coined by the Runnymede Trust in 1997 and suggests that critics of Islam are psychologically impaired (phobia is an irrational fear). It acts as a quasi-blasphemy law, and as a rhetorical device to deflect from Muslim discrimination against Jews, Christians and homosexuals.

94 Cockney , with its rhyming slang, is also a cryptolect, but of very different cultural purpose.

95 Chomsky N (2 July 2016): Why does the US support Israel? *YouTube*. https://www.youtube.com/watch?v=UotqG2avntM

96 *RT* (12 October 2017): British police accused of 'wasting time' as hate speech arrests up almost 900% in some areas. https://www.rt.com/uk/406467-hate-crime-twitter-troll

dangerous and even considered violent.

A common symptom of chronic schizophrenia is anhedonia, the inability to have fun[97]. Similarly, people afflicted with moralitis reject normal social pleasures such as humour, and attack the humourist. For example, after Nigeria was knocked out of the 2018 World Cup, someone amusingly posted on Twitter that the team had offered to compensate their supporters: airfares would be refunded on sending their bank account details. This referred to notorious e-mail scams, not unfairly associated with west Africa. Nobody believes that all Nigerians are involved in such trickery, but the joke was condemned as vile racism. Comedians, mostly left-wing since the 1980s, now find that their audiences pause before laughing at a joke, if it touches on any cultural sensitivity. Laughter, then, is not a paroxysm but a cogitated response.

Human beings are social animals and will seek comfort in numbers when they feel threatened. Jean-Paul Sartre observed the 'bad faith' whereby people deny their freedom, because it relieves them of responsibility[98]. As warned by Michelle Baddeley[99] in her book *Copycats and Contrarians*, a strong group mentality can be dangerous, particularly with the inflammability of social media. While well-intended, the #MeToo movement has invoked an atmosphere of summary justice akin to the witchcraft hysteria of the sixteenth century[100]. Jihadism is a herd mentality that was until recently allowed to roam free on the internet.

Christopher Lasch[101] correctly predicted before the turn of the century that the middle-class elite would become increasingly aggressive in defending its progressive ideology. Here are two instances as we were writing. When left-wing author JK Rowling criticised a court ruling against a dismissed employee who had stated that men who change sex are not real women, she was accused of transphobia and of putting vulnerable people's lives at risk[102] . Suddenly she became a figure of hate, an incredibly disproportionate response to the

97 Bentall RP (2003): *Madness Explained: Psychosis and Human Nature*. London: Penguin.
98 Sartre JP (1956/2003): *Being and Nothingness: An Essay on Phenomenological Ontology*. London: Routledge.
99 Baddeley M (2018): *Copycats and Contrarians: Why We Follow Others... and When We Don't*. Yale University Press.
100 *Daily Telegraph* (4 January 2020): Terry Gilliam: 'MeToo is a witch hunt'. https://www.telegraph. co.uk/films/2020/01/04/terry-gilliam-metoo-witch-hunt/
101 Lasch C (1996): *The Revolt of the Elites and the Betrayal of Democracy*. New York: WW Norton.
102 *Guardian* (19 December 2019): JK Rowling in row over court ruling on transgender issues. https:// www.theguardian.com/books/2019/dec/19/jk-rowling-trans-row-court-ruling-twitter-maya-forstater

moderate tone and content of her message. Rowling was hoisted by her own petard. Meanwhile on LBC radio, Iain Dale was presenting a debate on the taxi firm Uber losing its London licence[103]. A young female caller, rather than making her planned point, was enraged by the previous caller for complaining that many Uber drivers lack communication skills. Denouncing this perceived prejudice, she dismissed Dale's defence that it was reasonable for passengers to expect drivers to understand where they want to go. 'No, that's racist, he's being racist', she parroted.

The identity politics of race and gender are not merely undertones for those afflicted with moralitis, but always take centre-stage. For example, the women's fashion magazine *Red*, in announcing its women of the year for 2019, named three figures who were instrumental in blocking Brexit: Scottish nationalist MP Joanna Cherry, rich legal activist Gina Miller and Supreme Court president Lady Hale[104]. These women, according to *Red*, had stood up for democracy against trickster Boris Johnson. Having presumed that its readers were virtuous Remainers, the magazine reduced the biggest political controversy of our time to a feminist trope.

Similarly, when author NM was giving a lecture on risk management of psychotic patients under care in the community, race was brought to the fore by two white mental health nursing students. They were offended by the projected images of a lecturer who had been randomly stabbed, and of the disturbed young Nigerian man who had killed him. It didn't help that the report[105] was taken from the *Daily Mail*, that *bête noire* of the intelligentsia. The facts did not matter. An innocent victim's death was ignored. These students were more concerned with rejecting a racist stereotype. Soon they would be registered practitioners, making crucial decisions on patients' and public safety. Truly, people are dying as a result of moralitis.

---

103   LBC News (25 November 2019): Uber refused licence to operate in London by TfL. https://www.lbc. co.uk/news/uber-refused-licence-to-operate-in-london-by-tfl/
104   *Red* (January 2020): Women of the year. 33.
105   *Daily Mail* (8 September 2016): A tragedy waiting to happen: Man was FREED after assaulting a police officer and being found with two knives — just days before stabbing a much-loved lecturer to death on his doorstep. https://www.dailymail.co.uk/news/article-3779369/Man-23-pleads-guilty-murdering-renowned-lecturer-stabbed-death-doorstep-north-London.html

The breeding ground

As children go through school they are continually exposed to the liberal-left perspectives of the middle-class teaching profession. Child-centred learning theory suggests naturalistic personal development, but state-approved ideology is promulgated throughout. In 1997, Tony Blair set the priority for the 'New Labour' government as 'education, education, education', with a target of 50% of school-leavers going to university (this was eventually achieved[106]). Arguably, the aim of this policy was not primarily to increase academic qualifications, but to shape the social attitudes of the younger generations. Universities became finishing schools in a modernising agenda to 'smash the forces of conservatism'[107].

Since the 1960s, academe has been dominated by Marxist ideology, with whole faculties engaged in 'grievance studies' emphasising Manichean ideas of oppression and victimhood. But the problem of anti-conservative bias is endemic, reaching the top of the Ivory Towers. Everyone working or studying at a university is bombarded with virtue-signalling propaganda for favoured identity groups from the principal's office. Internal *communiques* are like an in-house *Guardian*.

Virtue-signalling value and special status are not applied fairly. White working-class boys are struggling in the education system, but their plight is ignored by the progressive establishment. When retired mathematician Sir Bryan Thwaites offered to fund scholarships for poorer white boys at two private schools, his bequest was rebuffed. According to Trevor Phillips, such squeamishness arises from a combination of middle-class guilt, inverse racism and misinterpretation of the law. For progressive school administrators, helping white boys would not contribute to diversity; instead, as Phillips[108] remarked, the idea probably conjured up images of the far-Right and aggressive English nationalism'. Meanwhile scholarships for black students are gleefully accepted by universities. This twisted morality has serious consequences for society.

---

106 *Daily Telegraph* (9 April 2008): Labour sticks to 50 per cent university target. https://www.telegraph. co.uk/news/uknews/1584495/Labour-sticks-to-50-per-cent-university-target.html

107 Speech by Tony Blair quoted by Boris Johnson (7 December 2000): Someone tell me what the fox Blair is up to. *Daily Telegraph*. https://www.telegraph.co.uk/comment/4257481/Someone-tell-me-what-the-fox-Blair-is-up-to.html

108 Phillips T (31 December 2019): Schools too afraid to help white boys; the Lakes deemed not ethnic enough… this lunacy helps no one. *Daily Mail*. https://www.dailymail.co.uk/debate/article-7838439/Schools-afraid-help-white-boys-lunacy-helps-no-one-writes-TREVOR-PHILLIPS.html

The university is an unwelcoming environment for white working-class males. The few who enrol are hectored about the 'patriarchy' by middle-class white women, oblivious to their social adversity. Campaigns against sexual harassment on campus always depict white men. And the vociferous (and officially endorsed) campaign to 'decolonise the curriculum' offends students who take pride in their national identity and heritage. While racism is highlighted as the great evil, traditionally-minded white men are insulted as 'gammon' (mostly by middle-class whites). So much for tolerance and diversity...

'Black History Month' is a well-intended endeavour for a more inclusive (and accurate) understanding of our past. Unwittingly, this is a form of *apartheid* pushed by a 'do something, feel good' establishment, placing a value on black contributions to history as a fraction of the academic year. But it has much wider implications. Radical educationalists are replacing 'pale, male and stale' playwrights and authors such as Shakespeare and Dickens with writers of African or Asian origin, and calling for removal of plaques, paintings or statues honouring benefactors or famous alumni. The Western scientific canon is criticised as epistemic hegemony. Narrative does not let the facts get in the way of a good story, as in the myth of Mary Seacole as a black founder of nursing (she wasn't a nurse, never worked in a hospital and wasn't really black)[109]. The campaign for removal of a bust of Cecil Rhodes at Oxford University[110] was merely the thin end of the wedge. Universities are hiring 'experts' to investigate past proceeds from the slave trade, inevitably leading to further erasure of historical figures, official statements of apology and a subtle form of reparations[111].

For anyone wondering where this will end, the answer is never: revolution is perpetual. The virus needs to mutate. As it evolves, it invokes new and more absurd ideas into public discourse. As there is limited social kudos gained from stating yesterday's opinion, the moralitic become ever more radical and extreme. Communism may fall, but cultural Marxism has proved resistant. Spread by moralitis, it will tighten its grip on society. Unless we act to stop it.

---

109   McDonald L (2014): *Mary Seacole: the Making of a Myth*. Toronto: Iguana.
110   *Daily Telegraph* (9 March 2016): Rhodes Must Fall campaign marches through Oxford: 'Standing here in the rain . we have thick skins'. https://www.telegraph.co.uk/news/uknews/12189390/Rhodes-Must-Fall-campaign-marches-through-Oxford.html
111   *Guardian* (5 May 2019): Bristol University to confront its links with the slave trade. https://www.theguardian.com/education/2019/may/05/bristol-university-slave-trade-history

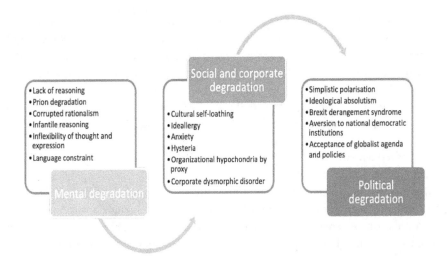

Diagram 4: The stages of infection: symptomatic degradation of the mind, society and country

Posing and policing on social media

The epidemic of moralitis is closely related to the rise of online social media. The younger generations use social media almost to the exclusion of face-to-face conversation. Most interaction by instant messaging may be mundane and apolitical, but the forces of conformity are constantly at work.

With rapidly developing technology, messages are imprinted amazingly quickly. The contagious bring new memes to the fore, and the mass of carriers transmit these as the accepted truth. A lie travels around the world before a corrective is issued, and who wants the boring truth anyway? Twitter became a perfect platform for identity politics, with its 140-character bursts of curt reaction and trite sloganeering. It is a humid swamp where the spores of moralitis multiply. Instagram is a boon for virtue-signalling, allowing users to align themselves with the latest cause simply by wearing a t-shirt or superimposing a love heart.

Whether in tweets or private chat rooms, all of these digital data are under control of the technology companies, which are using their growing power to take on the role of world police. In his satires, Roman poet Juvenal[112] famously asked: *'Quis custodiet ipsos custodes?'* (who watches the watchmen?). Not the

---

112   Juvenal. *Satires* (VI). *www.poetryintranslation.com/PITBR/Latin/JuvenalSatires6.php*

global social media companies, which collude with governments to eradicate problematic thought from their fora. Facebook founder Mark Zuckerberg[113] admitted that Silicon Valley is an 'extremely left-leaning place'. Moralising to the tune of identity politics is a lucrative cover for global monopolies such as Google. Although culturally progressive, their attitude to business regulation and tax is more of the libertarian Right[114]. In taking the moral high ground of the Left and employing a woke workforce, Silicon Valley hopes to evade state control.

Social media companies have fixed the internet to promote globalist liberal ideology and political parties that pose least threat to their expansion, while suppressing conservative opinion and inconvenient truths. The tech giants now face calls for regulation from the Right, which criticises their anti-conservative manipulation of news and information searches to reinforce their agenda and promote socially liberal politicians[115]. Ironically they have become a cartel against freedom of speech, deplatforming with the zeal of a militant student union officer. As propagators of the virus, social media companies are as toxic as a contamination of water supply.

Brexit mania: a severe outbreak of moralitis

When dawn broke on 24th June 2016 at the Glastonbury music festival, one camper summarised the mood by shouting 'Good morning, racist Britain'[116]. Brexit was a shock to the metropolitan elite and brainwashed youth, and this apparent resurgence of nationalism spurred fear and loathing. Expressing their horror on Twitter the BBC or the *Guardian*, previously rational and influential people seemed to have lost not only the referendum but also their minds. Known as 'Brexit derangement syndrome', this was an acute outbreak of moralitis.

Civilised middle-class marches with star-spangled flags and humorous messages presented a colourful and joyous scene, quite unlike the partisan football

---

113   *Washington Times* (10 April 2018): Silicon Valley an 'extremely left-leaning place,' admits Zuckerberg. https://www.washingtontimes.com/news/2018/apr/10/zuckerberg-admits-silicon-valley-extremely-left-le/

114   *New York Times* (6 September 2017): Silicon Valley's politics: liberal, with one big exception. https://www.nytimes.com/2017/09/06/technology/silicon-valley-politics.html

115   *USA Today* (10 April 2019): Ted Cruz threatens to regulate Facebook, Google and Twitter over charges of anti-conservative bias. https://eu.usatoday.com/story/news/2019/04/10/ted-cruz-threatens-regulate-facebook-twitter-over-alleged-bias/3423095002/

116   *Pitchfork* (28 June 2016): Glastonbury in the time of Brexit. https://pitchfork.com/features/festival-report/9909-glastonbury-in-the-time-of-brexit/

crowd atmosphere on heavily-policed Leave protests. The longest-ever queue at Waitrose, someone quipped[117]. But these self-congratulatory marchers, despite being of the graduate class, had little insight into their snobbery and no shame for their vandalism of democracy. Lurking behind the twee 'Can't get by without EU' and 'Never gonna give EU up' homemade placards was arrogance and contempt. Refusal to accept a fair democratic result was somehow justified by their moral superiority over the 'great unwashed'.

Author Ian McEwan[118] looked forward to over a million older people dying so that a second referendum would overturn the original result. Radio presenter Terry Christian[119] proposed that Leave voters be deprived of the influenza vaccine, so that they die sooner. Scientist Richard Dawkins[120] argued that the uneducated masses should be disenfranchised because they have shown their stupidity in voting to leave the EU. At rallies, MP David Lammy[121] repeatedly referred to Brexit campaigners as 'Nazis', doubling down on this when challenged. Labour politicians reneged on their own manifesto commitments and promises, in an ultimately futile effort to keep Britain in an undemocratic EU. Leave campaigners, according to Conservative MP Anna Soubry on *Sky News*[122], were 'fascists and overwhelmingly it seems many of them are racists', who need 'sorting out'. Does her incitement against political opponents, desire to overturn a democratic vote, and wanting this country tied to a German led Europe remind you of any political ideology from yesteryear?

For the younger generations, the EU has more cultural than economic value. This was shown by a survey conducted by one of the authors in collaboration

---

117   *Skwawkbox* (25 March 2019): The placards that speak volumes about the 'People's Vote' campaign. https://skwawkbox.org/2019/03/25/the-placards-that-speak-volumes-about-peoples-vote-campaign/

118   *Daily Express* (13 May 2017): Wait for them to DIE' Ian McEwan claims 1.5m Brexiteers 'in graves' will swing referendum. https://www.express.co.uk/news/uk/804111/Ian-McEwan-Brexiteers-referendum-Remain-sick-joke-Geldof

119   *Daily Express* (1 September 2019): Piers Morgan blasts Remainer's 'disgusting' tweet suggesting Brexiteers be denied flu jab. https://www.express.co.uk/news/politics/1172325/brexit-latest-piers-morgan-terry-christian-remain-tweet-flu-jabs-boris-johnson

120   *Daily Express* (30 June 2017): Fury as Richard Dawkins says British public is 'not qualified' to vote on Brexit. https://www.express.co.uk/news/uk/822870/Richard-Dawkins-British-public-not-qualified-vote-Brexit-eu-referendum-david-cameron-rt

121   *Guardian* (14 April 2019): David Lammy says comparing ERG to Nazis 'not strong enough'. https://www.theguardian.com/politics/2019/apr/14/comparing-erg-to-nazis-not-strong-enough-says-david-lammy

122   Soubry lost her seat in the 2019 general election. Nicola Duke (8 January 2019): Tweet. https://twitter.com/nictrades/status/1082616925547622400?lang=en

with economist Jonathan Portes[123]. A questionnaire on attitudes to Brexit was completed by 162 nursing and midwifery students at King's College London, of which 80.5% voted Remain. Respondents were asked for three words that symbolised the EU and Brexit to them. For the EU, most common were terms that expressed virtue, such as 'tolerance' and 'inclusiveness'. On Brexit, many respondents focused on the faults of Leave voters: 'xenophobia', 'divisive', 'backwardness' and 'stupidity'. The minority of Brexit supporters did not express doubts about the morality or intelligence of those favouring EU membership. The economy was scarcely mentioned by either side.

In their Brexit mania, bitter Remainers revealed much of themselves. The whole country was now privy to their posh dinner-party dialogue: they reject their own country and are ashamed of its traditions and heritage. Yet the liberal-left media give ample airtime to the Irish republican Sinn Fein and enthuse over the surge of its equivalent, the Scottish National Party, which wants to destroy the United Kingdom. Scottish nationalism good, British nationalism bad. Such anti-English prejudice in the upper middle class was a phenomenon keenly observed by George Orwell, but it is considerably worse than in his time.

It is remarkable that identity politics are so prevalent while national identity is banished. Nationhood should be the most inclusive of all, yet it is seen by the liberal middle class as regressive if not racist. Instead of celebrating Britain's tremendous contributions to modern democracy and human rights, the younger generations have been taught to loathe their country. In warped historical

123   McCrae N, Portes J (2018): Attitudes to Brexit: a survey of nursing and midwifery students. *Journal of Advanced Nursing*, 75: 1-9.

revisionism, national heroes are demonised: Winston Churchill, rather than saving us from fascism, was... a fascist[124].

After the 2019 election confirmed that the British people were as patriotic as ever, having been enticed by Boris Johnson's pledge to 'Get Brexit done', the liberal-Left was forced to reconsider its attitude to national identity. Perhaps this could be manipulated into something positive, as in the 'progressive patriotism', suggested by potential Labour leader Rebecca Long-Bailey[125]. But leopards don't change their spots. In the *Guardian*, Pankaj Mishra[126] was troubled by the appeal of Boris Johnson to people who should know better:–

> 'There should be no mistaking the neo-fascistic cults of unity and potency he promotes... Centrist dads as much as unteachable Brexiters are likely to invoke his much victimised silent majority of ordinary, decent men, dispossessed by immigrants and then gagged by politically correct academics and journalists.'

Fear and loathing

Cultural self-loathing will not end after Brexit. Peter Whittle, founder of the New Culture Forum think-tank, was spurred into producing the book *A Sorry State* after overhearing a chat in a bookshop concluding that England's most significant contribution to the world was the concentration camp[127]. Distinct from the admirable English quality of self-effacement, this nihilism extends to Judeao-Christian heritage and to Western culture and capitalism (although the critics like their mobile phones, and clothes produced in distant sweat-shops). Meanwhile the secularist *bourgeois* class has a hypocritical attitude towards other

---

124 *Independent* (30 January 2018): Boris Johnson calls on Jeremy Corbyn to 'denounce' activists who protested against Churchill-themed cafe in London. https://www.independent.co.uk/news/uk/politics/winston-churchill-cafe-blighty-finsbury-park-protest-boris-johnson-boycott-jeremy-corbyn-a8184231.html

125 *Guardian* (30 December 2019): Rebecca Long Bailey makes her opening pitch for Labour leadership. https://www.theguardian.com/politics/2019/dec/29/rebecca-long-bailey-makes-opening-pitch-for-labour-leadership

126 Mishra P (7 December 2019): England's last roar: Pankaj Mishra on nationalism and the election. *Guardian*. https://www.theguardian.com/books/2019/dec/07/englands-last-roar-pankaj-mishra-on-nationalism-and-the-election

127 Whittle P (2010): Introduction. In *A Sorry State: Self-Denigration in British Culture* (edited by P Whittle). London: New Culture Forum. 1-3.

cultures. According to Eric Kaufmann[128]. 'multiculturalism enjoins the majority to be individualistic and post-ethnic, and not to be attached to its groups, and minorities conversely to be attached to their groups'.

Cultural institutions such as the Proms are under attack from the very social class in attendance. The audience at the Royal Albert Hall is too white, and the classical music too Western! Recently the programme has been diversified to include rap and other contemporary sounds. Meanwhile British composers are marginalised, particularly if their work has any patriotic theme. Whereas connoisseurs applaud the Finnish nationalism of Sibelius, Simon Heffer[129] has highlighted numerous composers whose work has been neglected by the musical establishment due to their crime of being born on these shores. Edward Elgar, whose symphonies are unashamedly enjoyed elsewhere, is only known by musical snobs in this country for his 'Pomp and Circumstance', performed on the hideously jingoistic closing concert. Last Night of the Proms was the scene of Remain resistance after the referendum, with EU flags in abundance and slogans such as 'Thank EU for the music' (an adapted Abba song title making the dubious message that Brexit will stop orchestral movements).

This guilt syndrome is also found in climate change activism. It is often said that we have no right to tell the Chinese to stop polluting, after the West caused so much damage. Despite bearing placards warning of 'no planet B', protestors think that rapidly developing China and India are exempt, because they should have their turn too. A new coal-fired power station opens every week in China, where more cement was used in three years than the USA used in the entire twentieth century[130]. Factories and foundries belch fumes over cities, where the air is so thick with chemicals that it burns the throat. Middle-class 'green' campaigners know this, but still they would rather point the finger at the relatively low carbon consumer of Britain. James Delingpole[131] described

128   Eric Kaufmann interviewd by Isaac Chotiner (30 April 2019): A political scientist defends white identity politics. *New Yorker*. https://www.newyorker.com/news/q-and-a/a-political-scientist-defends-white-identity-politics-eric-kaufmann-whiteshift-book

129   For example, Simon Heffer (21 September 2019): Rediscovering Patrick Hadley, the forgotten genius of English classical music. *Daily Telegraph*. https://www.telegraph.co.uk/music/what-to-listen-to/rediscovering-patrick-hadley-forgotten-genius-english-classical/

130   *Washington Post* (24 March 2015): How China used more cement in 3 years than the US did in the entire 20th century. https://www.washingtonpost.com/news/wonk/wp/2015/03/24/how-china-used-more-cement-in-3-years-than-the-u-s-did-in-the-entire-20th-century/

131   Delingpole J (2012): *Watermelons: How Environmentalists are Killing the Planet, Destroying the Economy and Stealing your Children's Future*. London: Biteback.

'watermelons': caring green on the outside, but anti-capitalist red on the inside. However, like their schoolgirl heroine Greta Thunberg, most protestors lack insight to their Marxist manipulation.

Marxism is inherently destructive, and agitators often exploit the strategies of others to pursue their goal. Like Trotsky's mission of international socialism, the European federalist project gradually abolishes the nation state, which has been a brake on grand revolutionary movements. Of course, true Marxists have little love for the EU, they have seen how sovereignty and borders were successfully tarnished and weakened by the liberal-left education system, with no need for revolt. As Lenin described them, 'useful idiots' in the intelligentsia would do the Bolsheviks' work for them.

Cultural self-loathing is a symptom of a pathogen created in the laboratories of the Frankfurt School, fortified on the Left Bank of the Seine, and propagated by the elites in their quest for global control. Can this dehumanising sickness be cured?

Part III: Cultural remedy

The people are going to rise like the waters upon your shore.
A Donald Trump supporter[132]

Paradoxically, a virus must not be too virulent. A pathogen that destroys the host organism would kill itself too, making itself unable to transfer to other hosts. Moralitis is a germ that thrives in the educated minds of the middle class, but is this a sustainable habitat? On current form, moralitic liberal society will dig its own grave. Confused and neutered young men and ambitious feminists are not very procreative. This would result in a falling population, were it not for the liberal penchant for mass immigration, but the human tide of cheap labour mostly comes from regions steeped in conservative or regressive culture. Consequently, hereditary transmission of progressive values is weakened. For a while, institutions may be bulwarks of postmodern ideology, but these too will change with their human surroundings.

By inducing delirium, moralitis impairs procreation and thus reduces cultural transmission. However, it will continually evolve and spread into fresh fields where it can feed and multiply. New ideological battlegrounds produce new memes: today men declare that they are women; tomorrow marrying animals or inanimate objects? Progressive liberals cannot stand still or they will become conservative. Strains of moralitis will cause the host to internalise more absurd ideas. Yet by overreaching the virus becomes vulnerable to counteracting strategies, potentially leading to its extinction – or at least containment of the spread of the pandemic and reversal of the more extreme symptoms.

Like Soviet communism and all other grand schemes that defy reality and human nature, the subversive ideology of identity politics will collapse under the weight of its contradictions. Inevitably, conflict between identity groups has erupted, between feminists and the transgender lobby, and between Muslims and LGBT campaigners. After the election of allegedly misogynist Donald Trump, a million women marched in Washington wearing pink hats shaped like female genitalia. This 'pussy hat' movement flourished until it was reinterpreted as

---

132 Quote used as title of a book by Jared Yates Sexton (2017): *The People are Going to Rise Like the Waters Upon Your Shore: a Study of American Rage.* Berkeley: Counterpoint.

racist, because not all women have pink flesh. Furthermore, not all women have vaginas[133]. Suddenly it is exclusionary to use the term 'woman', and midwives (or, to be politically correct, 'birthworkers') must now speak of the 'pregnant person'[134]. Women's sports accommodate men who have changed sex in mind but not body: a development likely to cause consternation, and much mirth, at major events such as the Tokyo Olympics[135]. A woman who asserts rights for her biological sex risks being labelled as a 'TERF' (trans-exclusionary radical feminist).

Perhaps we should get the popcorn out, sit back and enjoy the various grievance groups fighting each other. But moralitis is too dangerous to take a Victorian *laissez-faire* approach. It must be tackled with ingenuity and vigour. The sick need treatment, and susceptible young people need inoculation.

Educational reform

From classroom to campus, the younger generations are immersed in progressive ideology, while conservative ideas are banished. Student unions ensure freedom *from* speech through 'no-platforming' and 'safe spaces'. Leftist prejudices are rarely challenged, such as the association of national identity with racism. Boris Johnson's government, with advisors such as free speech advocate Munira Mirza[136], should use its large majority to make real and lasting change to the moralitic educational regime. Of course, the 'Blob'[137] will fight back.

Schools are being drawn into mass canvassing for ideological campaigns. 'Learning packs' from divisive organisations such as the Muslim Council for Britain and the transgender charity Mermaids should be properly scrutinised and sent back if they are likely to do more harm than good. Parent power should be enhanced, reasserting the status of mums and dads as primary educators

133 *National Review* (11 January 2018): Feminists are ditching 'pussyhats' because they're racist and transphobic. https://www.nationalreview.com/2018/01/pussyhats-racist-transphobic-feminists-say/
134 *Conversation* (8 October 2019): How pregnancy can be made more difficult by maternity care's notions of 'normal'. http://theconversation.com/how-pregnancy-can-be-made-more-difficult-by-maternity-cares-notions-of-normal-117223
135 McCrae N (2019): Trans trouble at the Tokyo Olympiad. *Salisbury Review*, Winter, 30-31.
136 Mirza has frequently spoken out against censorship in universities.
137 Hunter M (24 September 2013): The Blob has run schools for decades: not any more. *Standpoint*. https://standpointmag.co.uk/issues/october-2013/features-october-13-the-blob-has-run-schools-for-decades-not-any-more/ An overly optimistic article when Michael Gove was the minister for education.

of children. Supposedly progressive changes to the curricula should be open to parental challenge, locally and nationally. Headteachers must take concerns seriously. It is imperative that facts take precedence over feelings, and universal values over minority-interest idealism.

Enlightenment values must be revived in universities, which have become *madrassas* of progressive ideology. Freedom of speech, democracy and equality before the law have been replaced by censorship, moral relativism and a pernicious idea that traditional attitudes are hateful. Universities should be rewarded for facilitating debate and nurturing diversity of belief. Critical thinking must be promoted over uncritically accepted dogma; reason over moralising; academic freedom over puritanism; and universal principles over segregating identity politics. These are not merely ideals, but a necessity for the credibility of our high seats of learning.

The younger generations, who are most susceptible to moralitis, need purposeful exposure to contrary opinions, ideas and evidence in universities. As a dialectic process, counter-argument should be presented for consideration and challenge. Seminars and workshops should use devices such as Socratic questioning and the 'Devil's advocate'. As Ronald Barnett (1990) argued in *The Idea of Higher Education*:–

> 'If we are seriously interested in developing a higher education in which the minds of students are really free, and do not succumb unwittingly to ideology, we have to develop, within the curriculum and within our institutions of higher education, reflexive strategies that encourage students to stand back from their core course of studies, see it in various perspectives, and take up critical stances towards it.'[138]

The decolonisation movement, which has built a head of steam in our universities, must be confronted for its divisiveness and hostility to national identity and belonging. It would not be exaggerating to regard this as anti-English / anti-British racism. This causes undue hurt for staff and students who take pride in their country, and who perceive double standards in how countries and their histories are portrayed. Inverse racism must be exposed for what it is.

---

138 Barnett R (1990): *The Idea of Higher Education*. Buckingham: Open University Press.

Student unions are a major target for reform. Under charity regulations, student unions are required to be apolitical, and officers should not attack staff or students for their political opinions. But they have become a law unto themselves. In 2018 Emily Dawes, president of the student union at University of Southampton[139], tweeted: 'Mark my words — we're taking down the mural of white men in the uni senate room, even if I have to paint over it myself.' The mural depicted scholars and students who served in the First World War. While the centenary of the end of this carnage was being commemorated, Dawes only saw white men to be sacrificed for emancipatory identity politics. Male rights campaigner Martin Daubney offered to pay for her to visit the vast cemeteries in Flanders fields. Her crass misandry was not dispelled by a grudging apology:–

'I had no intention of the tweet being taken literally, and upon reflection have realised how inappropriate it was. My intention was to promote strong, female leadership and not the eradication and disrespect of history.'

Facing reputational damage, Southampton University quickly distanced itself from Dawes' initial remark. However, universities have vicarious liability for the bodies that they host, and should be held accountable if they do not act on rogue activities. Like the destruction wreaked by trade unions in the 1970s, militant student unions are causing harm and must be reminded that their *raison d'être* is to represent the student body, not partisan activism.

As the think-tank Policy Exchange[140] urged in its report *Academic Freedom in the UK*, an inspectorate with teeth is needed to monitor universities and student unions, with a code of conduct to ensure staff and students are not browbeaten by censorship and propaganda. Penalties should be imposed on academic institutions for suppressing freedom of speech or proven cases of politically-biased recruitment, promotion or disciplinary action. Hit the Ivory Towers where it hurts.

---

139   *Daily Telegraph* (25 October 2018): Student union president causes outrage after vowing to take down war memorial mural because it contains only white men. https://www.telegraph.co.uk/news/2018/10/25/student-union-president-causes-outrage-vowing-take-war-memorial/

140   Policy Exchange (11 November 2019): *Academic Freedom in the UK*. https://policyexchange.org.uk/publication/academic-freedom-in-the-uk/

Relinquishing vulnerability and victimhood

Moralitis is curable by self-medicating on red pills,[141] available online. Yet this requires a degree of agency and a desire to see reality and escape from the woke intersectionality delusion. Younger people should listen to former US president Barack Obama, a messianic figure among woke millennials. Since he left office, Obama has criticised the attitude of this generation. Obsessed with purity, they act as if 'the way of making change is to be as judgmental as possible about other people'[142]. He observed that social media exchanges and campus culture have become extremely intolerant, with no room for redemption from social justice warriors who childishly cannot accept that the world is 'messy'. Harsh moralising dehumanises not only the target, but also the person pulling the trigger.

By policing every interaction and self-censorship, younger people are making their lives a misery. Sheffield University[143] announced its launch of training for 'race equality champions' to ensure racial equality on campus. These informers will snoop on students in the lecture halls, halls of residence and student union bar, reporting 'micro-aggressions' and educating offenders on how to talk to black people properly.[144] Examples of micro-aggressions to justify this woke policing included asking a student of Caribbean descent why she is frying a banana when it is actually plantain, and the awfully racist enquiry into 'where are you from originally?'

Consider a white middle-class girl, leaving home for the first time, and anxious to make friends in her corridor. Let's name her Sophie. She meant no harm by asking a fellow student about her cultural practices, but suddenly finds herself in trouble, having made someone a victim of racism. She will accept blame and learn to be more careful. But in private conversation with trusted acquaintances Sophie finds that they too been blasted in this moral minefield. However, we should not expect a sudden revolt by students. The doctrine of pervasive discrimination is embedded in young minds. The race equality officers in

---

141   A meme popular on the internet amongst conservatives and patriots derived from the 1999 film *The Matrix*, in which lead character Neo (played by Keanu Reeves) is offered the choice between a red and a blue pill by the rebel leader Morpheus (Laurence Fishburne). The red pill reveals the unpleasant reality, while the blue pill allows the recipient to remain in ignorance.

142   *New York Times* (31 October 2019): Obama on call-out culture: 'That's not activism'. https://www.nytimes.com/2019/10/31/us/politics/obama-woke-cancel-culture.html

143   *Daily Telegraph* (14 January 2020): Sheffield University to roll out training on 'micro-aggressions'. https://www.telegraph.co.uk/news/2020/01/13/sheffield-university-roll-training-micro-aggressions/

144   Joanna Williams (14 January 2020): Turning students into a woke Stasi. *Spiked*. https://www.spiked-online.com/2020/01/14/turning-students-into-a-woke-stasi/

Sheffield might say to unwitting offenders such as Sophie that society is racist, and that's what really caused her to make the ignorant remark. Consequently, both parties may be victims.

It has become widely accepted, albeit with limited evidence, that there is a mental health crisis in the younger generations. Universities have responded by channelling resources into mental health and wellbeing services and training for academic staff. The unintended (or possibly intended) consequence is that lecturers are deterred from discussing controversial topics for fear of upsetting or harming students. Indeed, mental health has been weaponised by the commissars of identity politics[145]. Children are being manipulated to fear for their future through ecological catastrophising and moral panic about nationalist dictators, while being misled into gender confusion. Older people are blamed for destroying the planet and prospects for peace. But an everyday danger to younger people is being scalded for innocent remarks by the woke enforcers of 'tolerance and diversity'.

In *The Coddling of the American Mind*, freedom of speech campaigner Greg Lukianoff and psychologist Jonathan Haidt[146] described three myths entrenched in younger Americans: the untruth of fragility, the untruth of emotional reasoning, and the untruth of them versus us. A victim culture has been nurtured by universities, where students are handled with kid gloves. Lukianoff and Haidt saw this 'safetyism' as counterproductive, arguing that 'if we can educate the next generation more wisely, they will be stronger, richer, more virtuous, and even safer'. In his *Twelve Rules for Life*, massively popular psychologist-guru Jordan Peterson[147] urged a shift from passive vulnerability to active responsibility and resilience. That is the route to freedom.

Contrarians are antibodies

Societies have a natural evolutionary propensity to produce contrarians who think 'outside the box', and who act as catalysts in overturning the *status quo*[148]. In our experience, while the white middle-class is straitjacketed by moralitis, students who break free from the chains tend be of other cultural backgrounds. Unburdened by guilt, they have licence not afforded to white

145 McCrae N (2018): The weaponizing of mental health. *Journal of Advanced Nursing*, 75: 709-710.
146 Lukianoff G, Haidt J (2018): *The Coddling of the American Mind*. London: Allen Lane.
147 Peterson J (2017): *Twelve Rules for Life: an Antidote to Chaos*. London: Allen Lane.
148 Baddeley M (2018): *Copycats and Contrarians: Why We Follow Others… and When We Don't*.

dissidents, who might be accused of insensitivity. Lecturers should support free-thinking students and allow them to challenge orthodox ideas. This will begin to expose the corrupted morality at the heart of cultural Marxism. As antibodies to moralitis, these students have the potential to unherd othes from sheepish conformity, and to push back the boundaries of progressive morality.

The first lesson for freshers is that everyone must be 'nice' to each other. But this is niceness distorted by moralitis and the imposition of ideological rectitude. Instead, we would say: stop being nice to people who are encroaching on your freedom and humanity. Stop being nice to people who claim to be tolerant, but who are extremely intolerant of opinions different to their own. If you have broken their rules, you are doing something right. The water is rising in the reservoir of offenders, and the dam will eventually burst. Contrarians are the antibodies that will reduce the incidence and prevalence of the disease.

Essentialism is extremism

On BBC *Question Time*[149]actor Laurence Fox spoke for the silent majority in defying the political correctness that normally emits from the mouths of panellists. Answering a question from the audience about racism against the Duchess of Sussex, Fox argued that such a charge is made so often that it is 'starting to get boring'. The university lecturer (an 'expert' in race studies) who had asked the question told Fox that he is a 'privileged white male'. Exasperated, Fox retorted:–

> 'I can't help what I am. I was born like this. It's an immutable characteristic. To call me a white privileged male is to be racist. You're being racist.'

In a later discussion of who should be the next Labour Party leader, Fox suggested the frontrunner Keir Starmer. When fellow panellist Lady Chakrabarti rebuked him for not choosing one of the four female contenders, Fox sighed and sarcastically revised his position:–

> 'Sorry, let me rewind. Any of the women. Is that better? Any woman. Because it's really important what your gender is or what your sexuality is rather than what your policies are.'

---

149 *Daily Telegraph* (17 January 2020): Laurence Fox says accusing him of 'white male privilege' is racism as he gets into Question Time row over Duchess of Sussex media coverage.. https://www.telegraph. co.uk/news/2020/01/17/lawrence-fox-says-accusing-white-male-privilege-racism-gets/

Responding to abuse on Twitter afterwards, Fox declared that the 'tide is turning' on progressive nonsense, and the episode was described as a turning point by conservative commentators[150], but few are as forthright as Fox. For all the people who agree with Fox, most keep their heads down in the office or the lecture hall. Otherwise they risk becoming genuine victims of a lynch mob or official sanction. Fox, for his misdemeanour, was castigated by the minority ethnic committee of the actors' union Equity as 'a disgrace to our industry' and accused of 'playing to the gallery' (an ironic criticism for an actor)[151]. Wokeness will always reassert itself, until moralitis is cured.

However, Fox made a significant contribution to the fight against stifling postmodern morality, by exposing a fundamental flaw in this way of thinking. In the past, egalitarians such as women's suffrage campaigners in the early twentieth century or the black civil rights activists wanted genuine equality, whereby a black person or a woman would have as much opportunity a white man. Fox explained that he was following Martin Luther King's ethos of judging people by their character rather than colour. But this is the opposite approach from that of progressive culture, which regards any criticism of a black person by a white person as racist, and any criticism of a woman by a man as sexist. This essentialism defines people by what they are rather than who they are. As Fox remarked, it is itself racist and sexist. Our inquisitors are not nice people at all — they are the extremists in our midst.

As the mouthpiece of the liberal-left commentariat, the *Guardian* is replete with perceptions of Britain as a hotbed of racism. But other mainstream outlets are little better. Recently author RO participated in a panel discussion on *Sky News* on a visit to London by Donald Trump[152]. He challenged Bonnie Greer, who accused Trump of energising a 'blood and soil' nativism and white supremacists. In fact, Trump and his 'Make America Great Again' slogan appeal to ordinary Americans – black, white and Latino. While liberals in California and Connecticut signal their emancipatory virtue, they were horrified when

---

150 Madeline Grant (17 January 2020: A challenge to woke orthodoxy that caught the public mood. *Daily Telegraph*. https://www.telegraph.co.uk/politics/2020/01/17/laurence-fox-question-time-perfectly-captured-backlash-against/

151 *Stage* (18 January 2020): Laurence Fox labelled a 'disgrace' to industry following Question Time race row. https://www.thestage.co.uk/news/2020/laurence-fox-labelled-a-disgrace-to-industry-following-question-time-race-row/

152 *Sky News* (3 December 2019): Panel discussion on *All Out Politics* (presented by Adam Boulton). https://www.youtube.com/watch?v=5K0DzFqXajY&feature=youtu.be

hip-hop celebrity Kanye West declared his support for Trump. A black man had stepped out of his pigeonhole, and was branded as a traitor. Who was really being racist here?

Reviving local and national identity

Nationhood has a bad name in progressive social circles, particularly as it is associated with the far-Right. However, Yoram Hazony's[153] *The Virtue of Nationalism* is a timely defence of the nation state. Although nationalism has at times been a malevolent force, more trouble has been caused by countries that attack and subjugate their neighbours. Nazi Germany was racist, imposing the rule of the 'master race' far beyond German borders; the 'socialism in one country' of the Soviet Union captured eastern Europe behind an 'Iron Curtain'; Napoleon, like the EU project, tried to impose a rationalist regime over Europe. These uniquely European ideas rejected the concept of the nation-state, giving primacy to transnational institutions over individual countries whose identities they tried to suppress. National identity is an enduring phenomenon, outlasting the designs of continental tyrannies. Indeed, it was the light by which freedom endured. Democratic nationalists stood up to and successfully overthrew these intolerant and totalitarian ideologies[154].

Hazony's five virtues of nationalism are democracy, individual liberty, collective freedom, banishment of violence and protection from imperialism. Legitimacy of the state arises from mutual loyalty, with citizens having rights and responsibilities. Tax is levied through a social contract: the NHS provides for all whatever their contributions, but health tourism violates the contract (as does extravagant foreign aid). Hazony concurred with John Stuart Mill's view of the state as ultimate guarantor of liberty, observing that 'nothing that has taken place in the subsequent century has given us reason to believe that his assessment is mistaken'. Hazony's concept of nationhood is more inclusive than the fragmentary identity politics of liberal cosmopolitans.

Patriotism is strong in the ordinary people but weak in the administrative core. Brigades of civil servants regularly troop from Whitehall to Carlton Gardens to hear expert speakers at the Institute for Government. This think tank, founded by Lord Sainsbury, is supposedly politically neutral but actually promotes a

---

153   Hazony Y (018): *The Virtue of Nationalism.* New York: Basic Books.
154   Philip Vander Elst (2008): *The Principles of British Foreign Policy.* London: Bruges Group.

globalist, pro-EU agenda that undermines national sovereignty. High-ranking officials relish the neoliberal gospel and the bypassing of democracy. In the 1970s television series *Yes Minister* a minister is always hoodwinked into taking the opposite action from what he intends by a sly senior civil servant. Sir Humphrey gets what he wants, overriding the manifesto commitments of the elected government.

The term 'deep state' was coined for the hidden hierarchy in Washington that really pulls the strings, restraining presidential autonomy and undermining American superpower status through a 'rules-based international order'. The liberal establishment, horrified by the great disruptor Donald Trump, comforts itself in the behind-the-scenes constraint on elected presidents and their appointees. BBC *Newsnight* presenter Mark Urban referred to this as the 'permanent government' of the USA.

A plethora of supranational institutions and agencies is governing by stealth. The annual gathering of the World Economic Forum at Davos brings together political leaders, media moguls, scientists, bankers and global corporations for macro-planning behind closed doors. Immune to the perils of plebiscites, these modern Olympians are steadily standardising and homogenising countries and their people into a global fiefdom with a pool of cheap labour and a market of woke consumers at the behest of a limited number of international brands[155]. Contrary to competition and diversity, this creates a rent-seeking regime, whereby the corporation best able to lobby for its favoured set of rules is the most likely to succeed, rather than whoever offers the best service or most value for the consumer. As Adam Smith[156] noted in *The Wealth of Nations*:–

'People of the same trade seldom meet together, even for merriment and diversion, but the conversation ends in a conspiracy against the public.'

Klaus Schwab, octogenarian leader of the World Economic Forum, is keen to harness the energies of youth in his grand global venture. Although Schwab would not say this openly, the young are being exploited by the climate crisis to foment rebellion against their nations. Ecological catastrophising carries

---

155   Minogue K (2004): *The Fate of Britain's National Interest*. London: Bruges Group.
156   Smith A (1776): *An Inquiry Into the Nature and Causes of the Wealth of Nations*. *https://www.ibiblio.org/ml/libri/s/SmithA_WealthNations_p.pdf*

the clear message that national governments are irrelevant if not negligent and destructive, and must be superseded by global action. As 'young people are right to be angry' about the mess that has been made by their leaders, Schwab argued that 'they should have seats at every table'[157]. The globalists are using intergenerational conflict to advance their cause: virtuous young versus selfish elders. Although the upcoming generations are described as more liberal than ever, they have been persuaded that more intervention is needed in every aspect of our lives. They are pawns of a progressively-cloaked totalitarianism.

Theresa May was strongly criticised when she used the term 'citizens of nowhere' for people who think beyond national identity and borders. She was accused, predictably, of giving succor to racists. But an important distinction should be made between civic and ethnic nationalism. The former embraces citizens of all backgrounds, while the latter is a morally suspect idea with limited support amidst a multicultural reality. The liberal-left establishment prefers to tarnish all national movements as a foot in the door for fascism, but most people are not racist in expressing pride in their country, or in wanting their government to prioritise the security of its own people. In an unstable world with mass movement from poorer regions, dramatic cultural change and the danger of terrorism and crime, it is not surprising that voters are turning to politicians who promise to protect them.

Patriotic movements are reinvigorating the nation-state, while centre-left parties that ignore a sense of belonging and the need for cultural security are losing. The Liberal Democrat party made a major strategic error in the 2019 general election campaign by pledging to revoke Brexit, despite this being the verdict of a referendum that the party had previously demanded. This was neither liberal nor democratic. Party leader Jo Swinson compounded this blunder by declaring her opposition to nationalism in all its forms, and by spouting woke ideas at every opportunity. She lost her seat to the Scottish National Party, bringing her political career to an early but deserved end. For politicians who think that national identity is an anachronism in a modern, borderless world the remedy should be simple: vote them out. However, we cannot vote out the hordes of bureaucrats and lawyers in supranational institutions, a globalist class that has waged lawfare against democracy and the nation-state.

---

157   Schwab K (3 February 2020): The world we leave them. *Time*. 44-45.

The media is the message, but the message is wrong

The BBC is frequently accused of talking in a metropolitan bubble, promoting progressive ideology such as transgenderism and 'climate justice' while denigrating patriotism and Christianity. The television debate show *Question Time* was dominated by Remainers throughout the tumultuous period following the EU referendum, with typically four out of five panellists opposing Brexit[158]. On retiring after a long career of public service, some prominent BBC presenters have used their newfound freedom to attack the progressive liberal bias in the national broadcasting service. Journalist Robin Aitken[159], in his book *The Noble Liar*, argued that the BBC has 'an agenda to destroy social conservatism'. John Humphrys[160], former Radio 4 *Today* presenter, remarked in his first *Daily Mail* column:–

> 'The barriers against the tyranny of woke should be manned by organisations such as the BBC. They have a privileged position as interpreters of the national conversation and they must ensure they are listening to it.'

Humphrys had been on the receiving end of several Twitterstorms late in his career, for offending gender ideology; for example, when he queried complaints made about an advertisement showing a mother with a pram, which was apparently sexist. He was called a 'dinosaur' for suggesting that generally babies are better looked after by mums. The thought police in the BBC are often quick to act against conservative personalities while allowing the likes of Jo Brand[161] to spout outrageous insults and seemingly incite violence in off-colour humour *ad lib*. However, the audience at home see through this bias, which is surely a major factor in Radio 4 losing listeners[162].

158 Joel Rodrigues (10 April 2019): It's official: Question Time is a Remainer stronghold. *Spiked.* https://www.spiked-online.com/2019/04/10/its-official-question-time-is-a-remainer-stronghold/

159 Aitken R (2018): *The Noble Liar: How and Why the BBC Distorts the News to Promote a Liberal Agenda.* London: Biteback.

160 John Humphrys (11 January 2020): Why has Britain lost its sense of humour? *Daily Mail.* https://www.dailymail.co.uk/debate/article-7875207/Why-Britain-lost-sense-humour-no-laughing-matter-says-JOHN-HUMPHRYS.html

161 *BBC News* (12 June 2019): BBC defends Jo Brand over 'battery acid' joke. https://www.bbc.co.uk/news/entertainment-arts-48611424

162 Ben Lawrence (8 January 2020): A tarnished jewel in the BBC's crown: what's going on at Radio 4? *Daily Telegraph.* https://www.telegraph.co.uk/radio/what-to-listen-to/tarnished-jewel-bbcs-crown-going-radio-4/

The BBC imposes a tax on all television users, but this model is anachronistic as younger people have moved online and drama is increasingly watched on internet streaming services such as Netflix. Despite its cherished status as a national institution, the BBC has weakened its public support by blatant political bias. Substantial reform is needed to ensure that the BBC is an impartial public broadcaster rather than a propagandist for progressive ideology. Otherwise people will justifiably refuse to pay for it.

Newspapers, in traditional or online format, are a major medium for progressive values. Editors decide what news to publish and how to report it, and in this respect they are serving their customers. Leftist intellectuals read the *Guardian*, while patriotic lower-middle class folk read the *Mail* or *Express*. But progressive values have reached far across the political divide. Beyond the news and comment in the conservative *Telegraph*, the reviews and features are increasingly tuned to identity politics, with articles focusing on race and gender as if these are the only considerations.

As most newspapers provide free content on the internet, printed news and supplements are at risk of extinction. The only newspapers that are widely read on the commute are free: *Metro* in the morning, and in London the *Evening Standard* on the way home. Writers in these publications seem to think everyone is either young, middle-class or both. Fewer people pick up the *Standard*, previously a newspaper of which Londoners could be proud, after editor George Osborne turned it into a mouthpiece for metropolitan elite Remainers, with smug columnists like Sophia Money-Coutts. Memo to newspaper proprietors: if you want to reverse the decline in readers and increase your advertising income, get writers who can talk to ordinary people, not Trump-bashing bores expressing their woke virtue.

Anxious to display their moral superiority, the movie business is a veritable well of wokeness. Demands for diversity in film award ceremonies are getting louder every year. Soon quotas may be introduced to ensure a gender and ethnic balance in nominations (which would become a misnomer). *GQ* magazine critic Sophia Benoit complained that the highly-acclaimed film *1917*, entirely set in the trenches of the Western Front, had no female characters[163]. Hollywood

---

163   Dan Wootton (17 January 2020): Stop all this silly hysteria… Brits aren't sexist and Bafta isn't racist. *Sun.* https://www.thesun.co.uk/news/10756125/bafta-isnt-racist-sexist-brits/

celebrities are insufferably woke in their acceptance speeches. At the 2020 Golden Globes film awards, *compere* Ricky Gervais[164] warned actors and actresses:–

'If you win an award tonight, please don't use it as a platform to make a political speech. You're in no position to lecture the public about anything. You know nothing about the real world… So if you win, come up, accept your little award, thank your agent and your God and fuck off'.

Through the instant medium of Twitter, narcissistic Hollywood celebrities just need enough rope to hang themselves. Actress Rose McGowan, who started the #MeToo movement against sexual harassment after her alleged abuse by director Harvey Weinstein, was enjoying a massive public profile when she pressed the self-destruct button. On 3rd January 2020, after Donald Trump had ordered the successful assassination of senior Iranian military commander Qassem Soleimani, McGowan tweeted:–

'Dear #Iran. The USA has disrespected your country, your flag, your people. 52% of us humbly apologise. We want peace with your nation. We are being held hostage by a terrorist regime. We do not know how to escape. Please do not kill us. #Soleimani.'

After seventy thousand mocking replies, McGowan doubled down with angry retorts such as 'Fuck your freedom'. Comedy cannot keep up with reality. In the puppet movie *Team America — World Police,* leading Hollywood actors took it upon themselves to negotiate a peace deal with North Korean dictator Kim Jong-Il, oblivious to his simultaneous masterminding of a global terror attack with jihadists[165]. McGowan and her ilk are a parody of their perceived higher plane of political consciousness, unaware of how silly they look.

Woke capitalism: resistance works

In 2019 Gillette, the leading producer of razors, thought that it would be a good idea to launch a marketing campaign alerting men to 'toxic masculinity'. This concept had been propagated far beyond the confines of campus feminism. For

---

164 James Delingpole (6 January 2020): Ricky Gervais deserves a medal for roasting the Wankerati at the Goden Globes. *Breitbart.* https://www.breitbart.com/politics/2020/01/06/gervais-deserves-a-medal-for-roasting-the-golden-globes-wankerati/

165 *Team America: World Police* (2004). Directed by Trey Parker. Paramount.

many years advertisements have depicted men as fools, and Gillette was taking this theme a step further. Here was woke capitalism: a company signals its virtue and gets praise in the media. But it didn't work this time. A mass boycott caused a sharp fall in share price, forcing Gillette to think again about insulting its customers[166].

Widespread commercialisation of radical movements indicates that morality has become as important as the material product. Why do train companies, for example, adorn carriages in rainbow colours during the month of the annual gay 'Pride' festival? Sexual orientation has no direct relevance to conveying passengers to their destination. Companies try to enhance their image by associating themselves with progressive causes, which they presume will increase profits. According to Clay Routledge[167], 'we are living in an era of woke capitalism in which companies pretend to care about social justice to sell products to people who pretend to hate capitalism.'

In ascribing to progressive ideology, companies are promoting conformity over creativity. The corporate world is becoming as intolerant as academe and the public sector in sanctioning employees or contractors who do not concord with the declared values of tolerance and inclusion. This destroys the potential of talented workers who bring genuine diversity to the company. But entrusting corporate ethos to young middle-class graduates schooled in woke ideology is perilous. One day's celebration of cultural diversity is tomorrow's cultural appropriation, as celebrity *restaurateur* Jamie Oliver found when he introduced his interpretation of jerk chicken, a Caribbean meal[168]. The spider's web of identity politics is best left to social justice warriors.

As shown by several highly-publicised feminist films flopping at the box office, progressive ideology is not always profitable, as will surely be realised by businesses whose corporate ethos is driven by a dozen purple-haired persons of gender fluid pronouns who think that the world is their Twitter echo chamber. When the *Always* tampon brand removed the female symbol from its packaging

166   *Guardian* (15 January 2019): Gillette #MeToo razors ad on 'toxic masculinity' gets praise – and abuse. https://www.theguardian.com/world/2019/jan/15/gillette-metoo-ad-on-toxic-masculinity-cuts-deep-with-mens-rights-activists

167   Quoted by Robert Oulds (2019): Why corporates virtuesignal: conscience or cover-up? *World Commerce Review*. https://www.worldcommercereview.com/publications/article_pdf/1517

168   Newsbeat (21 August 2018): Jamie Oliver's 'jerk rice' accused of cultural appropriation. BBC. https://www.bbc.co.uk/news/newsbeat-45246009

(because some men have periods too), a mixture of outrage and ridicule ensued. Companies should embrace diversity of opinions rather than reinforcing progressive group think. But most importantly they should go back to the basics of producing what customers want. Do not offend their sensibilities with the ludicrous tropes of subversive ideology. Go woke, go broke.

Protection at work

Like the Labour Party, trade unions have forgotten what they stand for. After a proud history of working-class emancipation, by the 1970s the large unions had tarnished their reputation with uncompromising militancy and self-destructive strikes. Accused of holding government to ransom, they were eventually confronted by Margaret Thatcher and came off worst[169]. Union membership has steadily fallen in Britain, although it remains strong in the public sector.

Millions of employees pay monthly dues to trade unions, as a form of insurance policy. They do so for two reasons: first, in the belief that if they get into trouble with management, the union will defend them; secondly, for the broader benefit of collective bargaining with employers on pay and pensions. While unions have continued to perform the latter role (to varying effect), the former is likely to disappoint[170]. This is partly due to the inherent conflict of interest in the system of representation. A shop steward is normally a colleague, but he is under the same management as the aggrieved worker, with his own career interests. He may compromise the worker or merely go through the motions, rather than get bogged down in a protracted dispute.

Failure of advocacy is worse if the worker offends both employer and union. This dire state of affairs has become increasingly common as trade unions have become fixated on progressive ideology and identity politics. For example, the literature of the vast public sector organisation Unison is dominated by anti-rascism and anti-sexism, to the extent that a white working-class male employee may not feel equally valued. The unions don't care, because such workers are a declining demographic segment: consequently, fewer low-paid white men are represented in the workplace. The unions are as bad as the Labour Party in their disdain for traditional values and patriotism; most of them campaigned against Brexit.

---

169 Moore C (2013): *Margaret Thatcher: The Authorized Biography, Volume One: Not For Turning*. London: Allen Lane.

170 Literally – in the past, the term 'disappointment' meant dismissal from work.

Imagine a bloke who speaks out when colleagues of like mind choose to remain silent. Let's name him Brian. He frequently gets into arguments with his peers about the EU. Brian's cards are marked, and when he makes an administrative error, he gets little sympathy. His career is imperilled, but the shop steward is a devout Remainer who has often disagreed with Brian on politics. Brian has made critical comments about mass immigration, potentially causing offence to members of staff of other ethnicities. Now he relies on someone who thinks of him as a backward-looking bigot. His shop steward will present a façade of ensuring fair process, but little more.

In a woke working culture, it is hopeless for a straight-speaking employee to rely on a mainstream trade union. For this reason, new bodies are emerging. The Workers of England is a recently-established association that is genuinely independent[171]. It deploys no shop stewards within the workplace, and covers workers in any field, from supermarket staff to lecturers. Some may fear that a general union lacks the specific knowledge of job conditions, but employment law applies across the board. Independent trade unions are thriving in the USA, where union membership is on the rise again after decades of decline. The Workers of England is likely to be the first of many new bodies that give workers the protection they need.

Another independent union was launched in 2020 by journalist Toby Young. Having personally experienced abuse and threats of violence at British universities, Young realised that at least he had the power to speak out. Most members of the campus community lack the influence to defend themselves against ideological persecution: they are easily cornered by the powers-that-be, and this includes the unions as much as the management:–

> 'Today, company managers and trade union officials have been to the same universities and move in the same elite circles and subscribe to the same woke orthodoxies on issues like Brexit, immigration and gender-neutral toilets. Union officials are more than happy to work with the bosses to weed out employees who don't share their progressive views.'[172]

---

171   Smith MLR (14 January 2020): The rise of the new unions. *Bruges Group*. https://www.brugesgroup. com/blog/rise-of-the-new-trade-unions

172   Toby Young quoted in Smith MLR (2020): The rise of the new unions.

The Free Speech Union will support members to the highest court of law. Successful cases will be a significant boost to academic freedom, something that universities have come to regard as a problem.

A statute of liberty

The function of parliament is debate and law-making, but many MPs seem to regard it as a virtue-signalling chamber. Politicians who wanted Britain to remain in the EU were unperturbed by the transfer by stealth of powers from Westminster to Brussels, because they do not relish such duties. They would prefer to display their progressive outlook and denounce sexism, rather than engage with different political or ethical views. In the Labour Party leadership contest in 2020, when it was revealed that nominee Rebecca Long-Bailey had listened to local Roman Catholic churchmen's opposition to abortion of a foetus with disability after the legal limit of 24 weeks, some fellow Labour politicians were enraged. European Parliament member Julie Ward[173] said: 'I cannot possibly vote for a person – a woman no less – who does not share my values'.

Since the rise of Marxist ideology, conservatism has been reduced to a passive or reactionary stance, always on the back foot. But this is beginning to change. Brexit and a heavy Conservative majority are a mandate for reviving British legal tradition, including common law, and reversing the encroachment of continental justice. We should revert to the principle that an action is permissible unless a law prohibits it, unlike Napoleonic legal culture whereby no action is permissible until a law allows it. Parliament should reinstate the Statute in Restraint of Appeals, which was originally drafted by Thomas Cromwell on behalf of King Henry VIII to forbid appeals to the Pope on religious or other matters, thereby making the King the final legal authority. Judiciability of the European Court of Human Rights should be terminated in England and by the devolved powers for Wales, Scotland and Northern Ireland.

Western society, far from being a bastion of liberty, is increasingly monitored by the authorities. With almost as many security cameras as people, Britain is becoming a surveillance state. This is merely the thin end of the wedge. Facial recognition technology will enable state snoopers to identify you from a remote

---

173 *Sun* (17 January 2020): Abortion row: Labour's Rebecca Long-Bailey sparks row with fellow leadership contender Jess Phillips over late abortion comments. https://www.thesun.co.uk/news/10757185/rbl-row-jess-philips-late-abortion/

watchtower wherever you go. Meanwhile, plain-clothed police officers mingle with the crowds at football grounds to catch anyone shouting 'hurty' words. The Stasi are in the stands. If middle-class virtue-signallers don't like tribal shouting and swearing at the stadium, perhaps they should go to an art gallery instead, and stop ruining Saturday afternoons for working-class blokes[174].

The law has been turned upside down by progressives in politics and the legal profession. When woke protestors are arrested, judges often side with them and set them free with a commendation for fighting for a good cause. However liberally the system acts, it is never enough for the adherents of identity politics, who see institutional racism lurking in every corner. Deportation of foreign criminals is anathema to woke activists. In 2018 Swedish sociology student Elin Ersson protested against such a heinous crime against humanity on board a Turkish Airlines flight from Gothenburg to Istanbul[175]. Having been in contact with the family of an Afghan asylum seeker who was to be expelled after a prison sentence, Ersson boarded the flight to try to prevent his expulsion. Her mobile telephone video went viral on social media, and her actions were celebrated across the liberal-left media as a heroine against European asylum policy. She received a modest fine for her trouble. In a similar protest at Heathrow, a deportation was stopped before a flight to Turkey[176]. Several passengers stepped in to rescue a Somali man, not knowing that he was a gang rapist. Perhaps that would have made no difference, such is the moral sickness. Stronger, exemplary punishment should be given to people who interfere with justice and thereby endanger public safety.

The Equality Act 2010, the last law passed by the Labour administration of Tony Blair and his successor Gordon Brown, has had profoundly adverse impact[177]. Equality is the sheep's clothing for a statutory wolf that attacks society with divisive identity politics. Arbitrarily defined groups are given special protection from 'hate speech', which is prosecuted on merely perceived offence. Sinister signs have proliferated in public places imploring citizens to report any utterance

---

174 Thomas Less (2020): Stasi in the stands. *Salisbury Review*, Spring.
175 *Daily Telegraph* (18 February 2019): Swedish woman fined for solo airline protest against deporting asylum seeker. https://www.telegraph.co.uk/news/2019/02/18/swedish-woman-fined-solo-airline-protest-against-deporting-asylum/
176 *Breitbart* (14 October 2018): Somali whose deportation was thwarted by passenger mutiny is gang rapist linked to ISIS fighter. https://www.breitbart.com/europe/2018/10/14/somali-whose-deportation-was-thwarted-by-passenger-mutiny-is-gang-rapist-linked-to-isis-fighter/
177 Kurten D (3 December 2020): After Brexit the next battle is wokeness. *Conservative Woman*. https://conservativewoman.co.uk/after-brexit-the-next-battle-is-wokeness/

mentioning someone's particular gender, sexual orientation or religion. This is not the Britain we once knew. The Equality Act must be rescinded as a priority.

The absurd concept of 'hate crime' should be confined to the annals of our unhappy period of postmodern legal activism. The police have no business in pursuing members of the public for political opinion or social commentary. A positive statute of liberty is needed in place of Orwellian laws and Kafkaesque inquisition. People should be protected from violence, incitement and breach of the peace but not from being offended. A revival of legal conservatism is needed to respect citizens as responsible adults. As a society we must decide whether freedom is a price worth paying for our supposed safety, which is really a cover for authoritarian control. Freedom of speech must be paramount.

Stop funding hate

Astonishing amounts of public money are given to groups that exacerbate divisions in society. For example, the Tell Mama charity urges Muslims and others to report instances of 'Islamophobia'. In the foreword to a report for the think-tank Policy Exchange[178], Labour MP Khalid Mahmood criticised the conflation of legitimate concerns about extremism with racism, warning that Islamophobia is being weaponised by groups of questionable motives such as the Muslim Council of Britain. The authorities, however, have fully accepted the term. Tell Mama has an interest in exaggerating hatred towards Muslims, as hate crime legislation is effectively used as a blasphemy law.

Another area where public funding is misdirected is the transgender lobby. Kathleen Stock is a courageous scholar who has been vilified for speaking out against the bullying and censorship of trans activists. Stonewall, the celebrated gay rights campaign group, is now focused on the T in LGBT, and its Diversity Champions scheme emphasises self-identity of gender, and hundreds of organisations have gained accreditation – at a price. Stonewall raked in £2.7 million in fees in 2018, funding training and consultancy for employers. But as Stock[179] explained, 'membership requires a host of further conditions upon institutional structure and provision that go well beyond existing law, and seek to control speech and attitudes about transgenderism and gender identity'.

---

178   Phillips T, Jenkins J, Frampton M (2019). *On Islamophobia: the Problem of Definition*. Policy Exchange. https://policyexchange.org.uk/wp-content/uploads/2019/05/On-Islamophobia.pdf
179   Stock K (2020): Sticks, stones and lawsuits. *Standpoint*, February: 24-25.

Government campaigns against hate crime are becoming counterproductive. In 2018 a poster campaign by the Scottish government and police upset Christians (see below)[180]. Barnabas Fund, an aid agency that supports people abroad who are persecuted for their faith, described the posters as 'state-sponsored hatred'. Use of the word 'sermon' was a clear reference to Christians. Several ministers of the Scottish parliament opposed the campaign for singling out Christians as haters. Investigating itself after formal complaints, Police Scotland concluded that the posters were not 'based on malice or ill will towards any social group'[181]. An independent body is needed so that oppressive and discriminatory interventions by the authorities can be challenged.

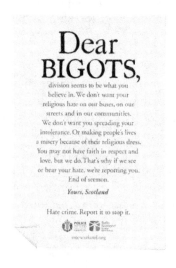

Humour is the best medicine

For many decades the stand-up comedy circuit has been dominated by left-wingers, who 'punch up' at traditional power structures. Jokes are rarely made about supposedly disadvantaged groups such as women or Muslims, as this would be 'punching down'. However, increasingly comedians have attacked ordinary, lower-class people, particularly on Brexit. Geoff Norcott was one of the few Leave-supporting comedians to keep his head above water while others drowned

180   *Times* (7 October 2018): Dear Bigots' poster upsets Christians. https://www.thetimes.co.uk/article/dear-bigots-poster-upsets-christians-h97hxsxvn
181   Barnabas Fund (18 December 2018): Police Scotland investigate and exonerate themselves over anti-Christian 'Bigot' posters. https://barnabasfund.org/en/news/police-scotland-investigate-and-exonerate-themselves-over-anti-christian-bigot-posters

in a sea of Remain[182]. Comedians who offend *bourgeois* values are unlikely to get gigs at major festivals or on BBC shows. However, there is a growing counter-culture on YouTube, where young viewers who tire of preachy jesters can enjoy ridicule of their puritanical peers[183]. Revolt is brewing: a bread roll was thrown at a prestigious cricket club dinner when politically-correct comic Nish Kumar[184] insulted his audience with some excruciating Brexit-bashing.

Like religion, humour is resistant to authoritarian control. Comedians are required to sign 'behaviour contracts' at some venues, to ensure that they don't tell any insensitive jokes[185]. But this concern is patronising. Supposedly vulnerable groups are not snowflakes; often any offence taken is contrived or by proxy. One of Bernard Manning's favourite gags was about his Asian neighbour in Manchester:–

'I'm a better man than you, Mr Manning'.

'How's that, Mr Patel?'

'Well Mr Manning, you have an Indian living next to you, but I don't have an Indian living next to me'.

When Channel Four sent him on a tour of India, the audience laughed heartily at this joke. In fact, Manning's neighbour was an Asian doctor who described him as a 'perfect gentleman'[186]. Certainly Manning told crudely racist and sexist jokes, but his gigs always sold out, with many people from ethnic minorities in the audience. If race and sex are as important to society as progressive ideologues emphasise, surely they are fair topics for comedy?

In 2018 the NPC (non-playing character) meme was spreading like wildfire on the internet. This reference to the background figures in video games

---

182 *Daily Telegraph* (6 April 2017): Brexit is a poisoned chalice for comedians — and as a Leaver, I should know. https://www.telegraph.co.uk/comedy/what-to-see/brexit-poisoned-chalice-comedians-leaver-should-know/

183 Marriott J (17 December 2019): The woke revolution is burning itself out. *Times*.

184 *Daily Telegraph* (2 December 2019): Nish Kumar met with boos and bread rolls for charity lunch Brexit jokes. https://www.telegraph.co.uk/news/2019/12/02/nish-kumar-met-boos-bread-rolls-brexit-joke/

185 *BBC News* (12 December 2018): Comedian refused to sign 'behavioural agreement' before gig. https://www.bbc.co.uk/news/newsbeat-46541002

186 *Manchester Evening News* (28 June 2007): Manning was no racist, says Asian neighbour.

characterised liberals as automatons. It worked too well: Twitter suspended 15,000 accounts, after complaints of trolling by supporters of Donald Trump or the far-Right[187]. This was a sense of humour failure by progressives who 'don't like it up' em'. The highly popular Titania McGrath spoof Twitter account lances the boil of puritanical identity politics, as in this tweet[188]:–

> 'Trans women are women. So why not just say "women are women"? Turns out the @PinkNews are transphobic.'

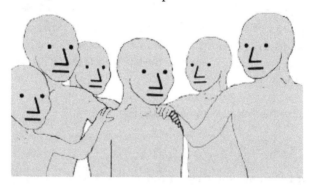

Postmodern ideology masquerading as science is another rich seam for satire. In 2017 Peter Boghossian, James Lindsay and Helen Pluckrose[189] had a series of bogus papers published in the journals of various 'grievance studies'. One paper explained the penis as a social construct, in the second the authors claimed to have examined thousands of canine genitals to reveal rape culture in dog parks, the third argued that men could quell their transphobia by anally penetrating themselves with sex toys, and the fourth was a translation of *Mein Kampf* with feminist buzz words. Other submissions were awaiting publication or review before the authors were unmasked. Amidst an academic backlash, Portland State University began disciplinary proceedings against Boghossian for unethical practice. The real ethical problem is in universities that produce fake research and charge student fees on a false prospectus.

Laughter, as the *Readers' Digest*, tells us, is the best medicine.

---

187   *BBC News* (17 October 2018): Why has Twitter banned 1500 accounts and what are NPCs? https://www.bbc.co.uk/news/blogs-trending-45888176

188   https://twitter.com/titaniamcgrath/status/1098910712435490816?lang=en-gb *Pink News* is known for witch hunts of critics of the LGBT political agenda.

189   *Atlantic* (5 October 2018): What an audacious hoax reveals about academia. https://www.theatlantic.com/ideas/archive/2018/10/new-sokal-hoax/572212/

Clinical assessment

The first step in the treatment programme of Alcoholics Anonymous is to admit to having a problem. As an initiation rite, the new member declares: 'My name is X, and I am an alcoholic'. In moralitis, however, self-awareness is impeded by the cultural pervasiveness of the condition. People will not see anything wrong with their attitudes or behaviour if everyone else thinks or does the same. For this reason, we have devised a short questionnaire (appendix A) for an indicative assessment of moralitis. Don't take this tentative effort too seriously, but hopefully it will be a precursor to a scientifically validated instrument.

Our questionnaire may be developed as a psychometric screening instrument to prevent further spread of moralitis in the organs of power. Soon after the 2019 election, Boris Johnson's advisor Dominic Cummings[190] urged fresh thinkers to disrupt the Civil Service, which is dominated by Oxbridge *bien pensants*. Root-and-branch reform is needed in recruitment and career development, with candidates assessed for their ability to understand the interests of ordinary people rather than the goals of liberal globalisation. Cummings wants cognitive diversity, but what we really need is better representation of the great British public.

Sequelae

This cultural virus will get worse before it gets better. Politicians, institutions and the media have invested too much in wokeness to suddenly abandon the cause. *Telegraph* columnist Bryony Gordon, who believes that younger people are suffering from a mental health crisis caused by older generations, is unhappy about the use of 'woke' as a term of abuse. According to Gordon, 'before wokeness there was political correctness, and before political correctness there was politeness'[191]. Be nice to minorities and all will be well. But as we have described throughout this book, political correctness and 'woke' are merely euphemisms for a warped authoritarianism that is severely constraining our liberty and livelihood.

Witch-hunters should be careful, because in future the boot may be on the other foot. But whether you are a patriot or a social justice warrior, a perpetual

---

190   *Civil Service World* (3 January 2020): Cummings seeks "weirdos and misfits" to work in No.10.
      https://www.civilserviceworld.com/articles/news/cummings-seeks-weirdos-and-misfits-work-no10
191   Gordon B (25 January 2020): 'Wokeness' has been weaponised in the war between Left and Right —
      and it ain't pretty.https://www.telegraph.co.uk/women/life/wokeness-has-weaponised-war-left-right-
      aint-pretty/

kulturkampf is a bleak prospect. Culture wars give oligarchies, whether of the Left or the Right, cover to pillage. Conflict between groups does not threaten their power. As the Labour Party seems unable or unwilling to learn, boutique activism and the licensed outrage of identity politics deny the primacy of economic justice. Arguably, the Culture Wars are employed to create factional distractions to protect the supranational order from meaningful reform.

As *Telegraph* writer Tom Welsh[192] observed, a 'permanent ruling class' is *in situ*, 'often internationalist, always metropolitan, and invariably woke'. This elite continues to dominate Oxbridge colleges, quangos, Civil Service, charity sector and our (or should it be their?) cultural institutions. Like bankers after the global economic crisis, they evade justice and retain their lofty and lucrative positions in the pecking order. Never forget that this imperious *bourgeoisie* created a Panopticon of state surveillance, denied our freedom of speech, and looked away as thousands of vulnerable schoolgirls were abused on an industrial scale by gangs of Pakistani men. And then they tried to subvert democracy.

Extinction Rebellion activists are a latter-day *krypteia*, displaying their moral superiority over commoners who work for a living. Founder Roger Hallam called for rationing, confiscation of property and tribunals akin to the Nuremberg trials, recommending a 'bullet for the head' for the worst offenders[193]. But in 2019, after a spate of highly publicised protests in London, these extremists were knocked off their pedestal. Or in this case knocked off the roof of a carriage. When two Extinction Rebellion protestors climbed on top of a packed underground train at Canning Town station in east London, in the morning rush hour, the station staff terminated the service[194]. Furious passengers shouted over the megaphoned sermons by the climate alarmists. They needed to get to work. One man got up on the roof and pushed the pair of protestors down to the platform, where they were accosted by the crowd. Eventually, when we look back on when the tide turned against woke ideology, we may refer to the Battle of Canning Town with similar prominence to the Battle of Cable Street, when Eastenders defied a different style of fascists.

---

192   Welsh T (19 January 2020): The bureaucratic blob is winning the long war against Brexiteers. https://www.telegraph.co.uk/politics/2020/01/19/bureaucratic-blob-winning-long-war-against-brexiteers/

193   *Daily Mail* (20 January 2020): Extinction Rebellion founder Roger Hallam calls for Nuremberg-style trials for people responsible for climate change. https://www.dailymail.co.uk/news/article-7906077/Extinction-Rebellion-founder-calls-Nuremberg-style-trials.html

194   *BBC News* (17 October 2019): Extinction Rebellion protesters dragged from Tube train roof. https://www.bbc.co.uk/news/uk-england-london-50079716

Imagine a world without moralitis. The germs have been eradicated, but subversive ideas have been wedged deep into souls. The landscape shows lasting effects of a condition that ravaged Western society: adults who have never learned how to formulate an argument or to cope with contrary opinion, thousands of victims of childhood transgender surgery, and European people a minority in parts of their own cities, the experience of Sweden coming to mind. But divisive identity politics and multiculturalism have been banished, as national identity and social cohesion return to the fore. Gender has been deconstructed and biological sex is back, with social and psychological differences between men and women embraced rather than denied. History has been restored, and the decolonisation agenda dumped: instead of wallowing in shame, Britain's tremendous achievements and talents are celebrated.

Most importantly, people feel free to speak. But for some, that liberty is hard to realise. Many years after the collapse of the Soviet Union, older Russian folk continued to censor themselves. Accustomed to a culture of fear, they would travel in silence, and speak to nobody that they could not trust. It was difficult to believe that eavesdroppers no longer straddled the corridors of their crumbling apartment blocks. The communist regime was internalised, lingering for decades in the minds of cowed comrades. The ideology that metastasised into moralitis may be similarly stubborn.

Conclusion

Should we let the epidemic of moralitis run its course? Time is not on our side. Social commentators Jonah Goldberg[195] and Douglas Murray[196] warn that Western society is in danger of committing cultural suicide. The woke have been radicalised, and it would be futile to treat them with reason alone. Taking a public health approach, preventative action is needed to arrest the spread of this destructive disease.

We recommend substantial reform to the education system, the civil service and other public institutions. Freedom of speech must be given due protection in law, with penalties for the silencers rather than the silenced. With Brexit delivered at last, the government should appoint a royal commission of enquiry into such

---

195   Goldberg J (2018): *Suicide of the West: How the Rebirth of Tribalism, Populism, Nationalism and Identity Politics is Destroying American Democracy*. Crown Forum.
196   Murray D (2017): *The Strange Death of Europe: Immigration, Identity, Islam*. London: Bloomsbury.

abuses of our *civitas*[197]. The main remedies for moralitis, however, will arise from people power: by shunning companies that insult customers with woke ideology, by voting for parties that understand and respect traditional values, and by challenging schools and public officials who preach subversive ideas.

As Sherelle Jacobs[198] implored in her *Daily Telegraph* column, let the wave of populism wash away false idols such as rapper Stormzy and teenage prophet of doom Greta Thunberg, who use their public platform to spread fear and loathing. These amplified demoralisers are beginning to irritate rather than persuade the general public. John Gray[199] commented after a series of electoral reversals for the liberal-left establishment that 'progressivism as a career strategy may be about to decline'.

Of course, the establishment will not relinquish power without a fight. The resistance will be smeared and vilified. But if we can win hearts and minds in the cause of liberty, society can recover from its moral sickness. As Mahatma Gandhi[200] reputedly said: 'first they ignore you, then they laugh at you, they fight you, then you win'.

197   McCrae N (8 October 2019): Time for a Royal Commission, *Bruges Group*. https://www.brugesgroup.com/blog/time-for-a-royal-commission

198   Jacobs S (2 December 2020): Time to shatter the false idols of our lazy elites. *Daily Telegraph*. https://www.telegraph.co.uk/news/2020/01/02/kowtowing-stormzy-greta-thunberg-exposes-elites-lazy-groupthink/

199   Gray J (2020): The new battleground. *New Statesman*.

200   *Quote Investigator*. https://quoteinvestigator.com/2017/08/13/stages/ Although the quote fits Gandhi's philosophy, there is no evidence of him actually saying this.

Moralitis Questionnaire

For clinical assessment and occupational screening

Please tick A, B, C or D for each question.

Q1. You overhear two men talking to each other in a pub, complaining about mass immigration. Do you: —	
A	Organise a multicultural flash mob
B	Condemn this as a Brexit pub and leave
C	Enter the discussion to consider the pros and cons of immigration
D	Buy the men a drink for the most sensible remarks you've heard all day

Q2. How should the demographic profile of Members of Parliament be determined?	
A	Quotas for ethnicity, sex and sexual orientation to ensure diversity
B	Targets for ethnicity, sex and sexual orientation to promote diversity
C	All-women, all-black / Asian and all-LGBT shortlists for party canidates
D	Whoever voters choose

Q3. A right-wing provocateur has been invited on to *Question Time*. Do you: —	
A	Sign a petition against the BBC for 'normalising fascism'
B	Watch the show hoping to see the offending panellist ridiculed
C	Watch the show with genuine interest in the debate
D	Applaud the BBC for asserting freedom of speech and diversity of opinion

Q4. A ruling by the European Court of Human Rights decrees that all professional men's and women's sports teams must be open to transgender players. Do you: —	
A	Call for a boycott of any club that mixes men and women in its teams
B	Laugh this off as the latest absurdity of identity politics
C	Accept the new reality that players are whatever they want to be
D	Celebrate this progressive overturning of gender stereotypes

Q5. An animal rights stall in the high street is asking the public what concerns them most. Is your biggest concern:–

A	Equality of human and animal rights
B	Clothes made of sheep or alpaca wool
C	Foxhunting
D	Halal butchery without stunning

Q6. For how many of the letters in the LGBT+ formulation do you know the meaning?

A	Three or less
B	Four
C	Five to seven
D	Eight or more

Q7. A university has embraced a programme of 'decolonisation', and you are invited to contribute to a working party. Do you: —

A	Suggest a more valid representative be found from an oppressed group
B	Agree to attend a session to offer your contribution to a worthy cause
C	Decline the invitation, suggesting a road to hell paved with good intentions
D	Alert a newspaper to this subversive activity in a seat of learning

Q8. An athlete of African or Asian background has won the BBC prize for sportsperson of the year. What is your response?

A	See this as a sting in the eye for racist bigots
B	Celebrate this as a success of multiculturalism
C	Think nothing of ethnicity and admire the athletic talent
D	Grumble about inverse racism

Q9. Department of Education guidance has been issued to schools, recommending a sanitary towel bin in the boys' toilets. How do you respond?

A	Write to your MP and the headteacher about the dangers of transgenderism
B	Ridicule this policy on social media as further evidence of liberal madness
C	See this provision as no real problem
D	Applaud this progress and encourage your work / university to do the same

Q10. A comedian is asked to sign a 'behaviour agreement' before a gig at a student union. How do you see this?

A	A step forward in banning hate speech
B	Relief that students can attend without fear of being offended
C	There are likely to be fewer laughs
D	The event will become a show of political correctness instead of comedy

Q11. The Hungarian government has been warned that if protestors are killed by heavy-handed police, the EU army will be sent into Budapest. What do you think?	
A	A pan-European protest should be organised against this invasion
B	This is a worrying repeat of the Soviet Union's action in 1956
C	The EU has a responsibility to protect its citizens
D	The Hungarian government should be replaced by a EU administration

Q12. Your work / university Christmas party has been renamed 'end-of-year' party? How do you react?	
A	Blame this on excessive sensitivity to other faiths
B	Ask the organisers to reconsider
C	See no problem as it's still a party
D	Approve of this as it shows sensitivity to people of other faiths or none

Scoring

Question	A	B	C	D
1	3	2	1	0
2	3	2	1	0
3	3	2	1	0
4	0	1	2	3
5	3	2	1	0
6	0	1	2	3
7	3	2	1	0
8	3	2	1	0
9	0	1	2	3
10	3	2	1	0
11	0	1	2	3
12	0	1	2	3

Overall score

0-11: symptom-free – you are likely to be labelled 'far-right'
12-23: not diagnosable — you will be asked to attend diversity training
24-29: mild case – you conform to progressive ideology, but check your privilege
30-36: severe case – a rewarding career awaits you in a woke organisation

Rebutting the Wigston Report

A Response to the Ministry of Defence 'Report on Inappropriate Behaviours' in the Armed Services

Introduction

Over the top they go, through the gaps in the barbed wire, to launch their attack. Spaced out like a line of ducks in a shooting gallery, they proceed at strictly walking pace over shell-blasted no-man's land. A sergeant follows them with pistol cocked, ready to dispatch any man dragging his heels. Soon they are mown down by a Maxim machine gun, and few reach the opposing trenches.

More than a century after the horrors of the trenches, the sacrifice of generations of young men continues to be honoured on the annual day of remembrance. The crowds at such ceremonies are growing, as a society living in relative comfort looks back in bewilderment and admiration at the courage of a doomed youth. The Help for Heroes charity has received generous support, partly due to public dismay at the neglect of ex-servicemen by the state. For all the talk today of a mental health crisis in younger people, they won't be conscripted to a rat-infested, shrapnel-splayed existence in the Flanders mud, dodging the sting of death.

Today, the armed services are not engaged in a major conflict, but they face a new threat from within. The Army, Royal Navy and RAF have always had strict discipline, ensuring their efficiency and effectiveness as fighting forces at the ready. But in 2019, following numerous media reports of discrimination and harassment by serving members of the armed forces, the Secretary of State for Defence commissioned an urgent enquiry into 'inappropriate and allegedly unlawful behaviours'.

The resulting report by Air Chief Marshal Michael Wigston CBE (known as the Wigston Report) starts from the premise that the standard of behaviour expected of service personnel is higher than that of the society they serve. Inappropriate behaviours are defined as 'breaches of laws, norms of behaviour or core values and standards which harm or risk harming individuals, teams or operational effectiveness and that bring or risk bringing the reputation of individuals, units, the Service or Defence into disrepute'. Whether these occur due to stress and low morale in services of steadily reducing strength, or the devil making work for idle hands, the report emphasised:–

> The judgement we expect of our people on the battlefield must be the same level of judgement that we expect of that behaviour in the barrack block or the bar'.

The Armed Forces Continuous Attitudes Survey in 2018 showed that while the majority of servicemen and servicewomen were satisfied with their working conditions and relationships, 12% had experienced bullying, harassment or discrimination in the past year (6% having reported these incidents). Risk factors, according to the Wigston Report, include: 'tight-knit units that perceive themselves as elite; masculine cultures with low gender diversity; rank gradients; age gradients; weak or absent controls, especially after extensive operational periods; and alcohol'.

This response to the Wigston Report considers the potential impact of its wide-reaching recommendations on morale and military effectiveness.

Diversity and discrimination

The armed services are striving to become more reflective of society, attracting more women, members of black or Asian communities, and people who identify themselves as LGBT (lesbian, gay, bisexual and transgender). A recent recruiting campaign by the Army, 'Keeping my Faith', depicted a Muslim soldier on a prayer mat, taking a break from patrol as his comrades respectfully stand aside (*Daily Mail*, 14 January 2018). Another advertisement appealed to 'snowflakes', a disparaging label for younger people who feel threatened or traumatised by contrary opinions. Like in many civil organisations, the mantra of diversity has seemingly become as much of a priority as the *raison d'être* of the service. The rationale seems to be that 'what we do' depends on 'who we are'.

As the demographic profile of the armed services has changed, bullying and harassment have been disproportionately reported by female, homosexual and black or Asian personnel. There may also be under-reporting due to fear of not being believed by biased or insensitive superiors. The number of sexual offences investigated by military police has steadily increased, with women accounting for 82% of victims. Unquestionably, women should be protected from sexual harassment; personnel of black and Asian heritage should not tolerate racial discrimination; and gay men and lesbians have a right to their sexual orientation without prejudice. It is the experience of these groups that causes most concern for the Wigston Report.

A key recommendation of the report is to establish 'a Defence Authority responsible for cultures and Inappropriate Behaviours' (*sic*). This centralised structure will set standards for monitoring behaviour and introduce a complaints system with 'modern reporting methods' (e.g. instant messaging applications). It will be a hungry beast:–

> 'In order to provide the oversight and governance required, the Authority will need to be fully resourced with suitably qualified and experienced people otherwise it will not make a difference. We estimate around 30-50 people will be required.'

This raises the troubling prospect of an Orwellian structure for disciplining and ejecting blokes who don't adequately display the favoured values of tolerance and diversity. Many a strong character, and the type of person you'd want beside you in a situation of grave danger, could be booted out for using wrong words in the mess. Since the MacPherson Report into the racist murder of black teenager Stephen Lawrence, organisations in fear of being accused of institutional racism have accepted the concept of a racist incident as anything that is perceived as racist (*Daily Telegraph*, 24 February 2009) . The same applies to sexism and other perceived prejudices against minority groups.

Although the Wigston Report sometimes uses the prejudicial terms of 'victim' and 'perpetrator', generally it refers to 'complainants'. This sensible wording may have been influenced by the scandal of Carl Beech, a paedophile fantasist whose tales of systematic child sexual abuse by prominent politicians and other figures were ludicrously declared as 'credible and true' by the Metropolitan Police, leading to a costly investigation that tormented innocent men and their families. Yet the idea that the victim should be believed has taken hold in our judiciary, police and public institutions. The report lauds the #MeToo movement, its dramatic impact showing that society is 'becoming much less tolerant of inappropriate behaviour in any environment'. The onus of proof has shifted from the accuser to the accused, the latter guilty until proved innocent. Disbelieving a complaint is wrong, but so is a presumption of truth.

Changing culture and behaviour

Mandatory training is regarded as essential to changing the culture. The Wigston Report has clearly consulted the equality and diversity phrasebook. There is emphasis on revealing and correcting 'unconscious bias', which means 'learned stereotypes that are automatic, unintentional, deeply engrained, universal and able to influence behaviour'. With much work to be done, the report recommends 'immersive value-based training'.

The report uses the anti-racism term of 'micro-aggressions', defined in the glossary as 'brief and commonplace daily verbal, behavioural, or environmental indignities, whether intentional or unintentional, that communicate hostile, derogatory, or negative prejudicial slights and insults towards any individual or group'. These hostile acts 'pass unrecognised by those who have committed them'. With constant vigilance, such behaviour will be nipped in the bud:–

> 'An inappropriate comment is made, a corporal tells the perpetrator to apologise, explaining why it caused offence, the apology is made and accepted, and the matter resolved.'

This sequence is neat on paper, but would it always work in practice? This simplistic intervention raises several questions:–

1 Is being ordered to apologise likely to produce a genuine apology?

2 What if the person being told to apologise does not think that he's done anything wrong?

3 What if the person receiving an apology did not feel offended (perhaps having engaged in harmless banter)?

4 Does the corporal accept an offence as it was perceived, or is he the arbiter of whether it is worthy of apology?

5 What if the offending comment was a response to a provocative comment by the other person?

6 Would the incident be recorded in the offending person's file, and the corporal's virtuous intervention noted?

No man's land

The evolving culture in the armed services could be creating a minefield for young men, particularly those of traditional working-class background – black or white. Their very maleness is now being seen as a problem, rather than a positive attribute. Terms once restricted to radical sociology departments in second-rate universities such as 'toxic masculinity', 'white privilege', 'mansplaining' and 'the patriarchy' are now regular features of the armed services' modernising discourse. The top brass has embraced 'woke' ideology, and hitherto-valued attributes such as strength, stoicism and competitiveness are treated with suspicion.

The quest is not just for brain over brawn, but a total reconstitution of personnel: working-class men must no longer be the mainstay. The report enthuses that 'our new generation, which includes a greater proportion of BAME, women and other underrepresented groups, has grown up in a more open and permissive society.' But this is muddled thinking: armed units should be cohesive and disciplined rather than 'open and permissive'. Indeed, the report itself is opposed to licentiousness, and rather than openness it supports anonymity (of the accuser but not the accused).

Diversity is prioritised – but at what cost? As Douglas Murray (2019) wrote in his polemic *The Madness of Crowds*, the idea of harmful masculinity has gone mainstream without scientific validation or rational critique. In pseudo-scientific virtuousness the American Psychological Association (2019) diagnosed traditional masculinity as a syndrome featuring 'anti-femininity, achievement, eschewal of the appearance of weakness, and adventure, risk and violence.' Few scholars would dare to challenge the feminist onslaught. Steven Pinker's excoriating tome *The Blank Slate* (2002) should have ended the postmodern delusion that all differences between the sexes are due to social learning, but as witnessed with communism, facts are not allowed to stand in the way of revolutionary truth. Murray queried the concept of toxic masculinity:–

'When is that competitiveness toxic or harmful, and when is it useful? Might a male athlete be allowed to use his competitive instincts on the racetrack? If so how can he be helped to ensure that off the track he is as docile as possible? Might a man facing inoperable cancer with stoicism be criticized for doing so, and helped out of this harmful position into a situation in which he demonstrates less stoicism? If 'adventure' and 'risk' are indeed male traits then when and where should men be encouraged to drop them? Should a male explorer be encouraged to be less adventurous, a male firefighter be trained to take fewer risks? Ought male soldiers be encouraged to be less connected to 'violence' and be keener to show an appearance of weakness?'

Camp Bastion

Do women bring something unique to the armed services, either by nature or nurture? Do gay men too? Possibly, but these are sensitive questions, and any observed differences (whether or not scientifically tested) should be extrapolated with caution. Essentialism is selectively applied by progressive policy-makers: a flawed and discriminatory concept in some situations, but applied without qualification when it suits. Previously disadvantaged groups can have their cake and eat it. Having deservedly gained equality in law, campaigners now claim special rights. Murray (2019), himself a gay man, suggested that some homosexual men 'want to be precisely equal but with a little gay bonus'.

The pursuit of identity politics are not merely to gain rights, but also a projection of superiority. Evidence shows that gay men and lesbians fare better than heterosexuals in the job market, at least in the USA (*Vice News*, 14 September 2017), perhaps because they are better at navigating the modern social and occupational landscape. But gay talent may be misdirected, as with the notorious Cambridge Spy Ring (Volkman, 1995). Similarly, there is a subtle (and often blatant) message that women do jobs better than men: arguably they are more conscientious, more emotionally intelligent, more supportive of colleagues and often more educated.

Swallowing Amazons

A survey of 3,000 men and women by Hive, a project management software company, indicated that female workers are more productive than male colleagues

(*World Economic Forum*, 8 October 2018). Hive's *State of the Workplace Report* showed that while both sexes complete about 66% of their tasks, women are assigned 10% more work than men, and consequently they are more industrious. The report suggested that men avoid tasks that gain little reward, with female staff taking up the slack. This may be true of office environments, but how does it relate to the armed services?

An American study (Novak, Brown & Frank, 2011) showed that female police officers are less likely than male colleagues to arrest suspects, which was lauded as evidence that women are better at handling conflict. But instead, could it be that they lacked the physical prowess to arrest someone safely? The same study showed that policewomen were more likely to arrest in the presence of their supervisors.

Female leaders are as capable of disastrous decisions as male duffers. For example, Metropolitan Police Commissioner Cressida Dick presided over the disastrous handling of the sexual abuse allegations against prominent figures by Carl Beech. The ensuing witch hunt was influenced by the feminist notion of 'believe the victim', endorsed by the Metropolitan Police on Dick's watch. Eventually, after several miscarriages of justice, Dick reversed this policy (*Times*, 2 April 2018). Dany Cotton, female chief of the London Fire Brigade, failed to order evacuation of the blazing Grenfell Tower (*Daily Mail*, 27 September 2018). Again, this is not directly attributable to sex or gender, but women tend to be more risk-averse than men (although some female leaders throw caution to the wind, Margaret Thatcher coming to mind). Cotton persisted with the 'stay-put' policy for high-rise buildings, prioritising the safety of her firefighters over their life-saving imperative. At the enquiry into the tragedy in which 71 people perished, Cotton unrepentantly said:–

> 'I wanted those firefighters to have a positive reinforced memory before they went into the building of somebody saying nice things to them, being supportive and demonstrating to them that somebody really cared.'

To be fair, many disasters may be attributed to male traits of risk-taking and territorial aggression. But leadership in the armed services requires direct experience and awareness of how men behave in battle conditions, and appointment of women to senior positions may bypass this journey. The push for equality is a denial of the observable truth that some jobs are likely to be done better by women, while other vocations are more tuned to male attributes. Arguably, soldiering is as masculine as midwifery is feminine. There may be exceptions in male midwives and female soldiers, and equality legislation protects these opportunities. But there is concern that making the Army more female-friendly is reducing military effectiveness. There is an evolutionary background to male risk-taking: its attractiveness to the female of the species increases the chance of transmission of this characteristic in the gene pool[201].

Women on the frontline

Soldiering often entails a peace-keeping role, but sometimes it demands aggression and a killer instinct. Troops must be able to fight strong and determined enemy men. Colonel Tim Collins argued in the conservative *Daily Telegraph* (10 July 2016):–

> 'The infantry is no place for a woman, and to permit them to serve in close combat roles is a pure politically correct extravagance. No one pretends that allowing women onto the front line enhances the Army's capabilities; of the 7,000 women serving in the British Army today, only about 5 per cent would even pass the physical entry tests, according to the Forces' own research.'

The Army should be wary of lowering entrance criteria for women, as has been done in the fire brigade and police. In 2015 a study by the United States Marine Corps of the introduction of women into combat units found the performance of mixed-sex groups on infantry tasks was almost a third lower than that of all-male groups. Not surprisingly women proved physically weaker; they could not carry heavy packs on long marches and could not lift male colleagues when required. The study report concluded that units' combat effectiveness would be reduced; consequently, this recruitment policy risks lives on the battlefield. Collins ridiculed comparisons to other countries with mixed-sex armies:–

> 'Those who advocate this mistake for the British Army – usually failed male politicians with no military knowledge, but desperate to be seen as right-on – point to how it has "worked" on the Continent,

---

201   Habig B, Chiyo PI, Lahti DC (2017): Male risk-taking is related to number of mates in a polygynous bird. *Behavioral Ecology*, 28: 541-548.

without acknowledging that, with the possible exception of France, European militaries these days are essentially large 18-30, Club Med-style organisations with a vaguely military theme, requiring of their recruits only aggressive camping.'

Also writing in the *Telegraph* (5 April 2016), Colonel Richard Kemp, who commanded British forces in Afghanistan, issued a pronounced warning against female soldiers:–

'This is an extremely dangerous move. Physical fitness is the single most important building block for an infantry soldier. Everything else depends on it. The only people who fully understand the demands of infantry close combat are infantrymen themselves. I have not heard a single serving or retired infantryman say that admitting women is the right thing to do – unless their wives or senior officers are listening. The overwhelming majority are vehemently opposed and many have said that if women join they will leave.'

Kemp explained that feelings run so high on this 'because every infantryman knows that the price for this social engineering experiment will be paid in blood'. Technology has diminished heavy manual work in many occupations, including some parts of the armed services, but the demands on foot soldiers have not changed for a hundred years:–

'Infantry soldiers must still be able to march for miles over harsh terrain in searing heat, bent under the weight of 100 pounds of combat equipment, and then fight face-to-face with a ruthless, tough and determined enemy.'

The Army's own research shows that women are twice as likely as men to be injured in training. Kemp asked:–

'Aside from the physical and mental ability of female infantry to overcome and kill male enemy soldiers at close quarters with bayonet, boot and fist, why risk our soldiers becoming casualties on an arduous approach march or long-range combat patrol? Through no fault of their own, women will often become the weak link in an infantry team. The men will have to take up the slack and this will engender resentment and reduce the cohesion that is so vital for effective infantry combat.'

Finally, Kemp worried that physical limitations and injuries suffered by women would lead to softening of the tough training needed for combat:–

> 'Even in the tranquillity of a peacetime barracks, three RAF women sustained spinal and pelvic injuries due to over-striding to keep pace with the men on parade. They were awarded £100,000 each. The RAF's remedy was to shorten stride-length and place women at the front of the squad to set a reduced pace for the men – an ominous indication of things to come for the infantry.'

A point not made by Kemp or Collins, but highly relevant to the *Inappropriate Behaviours* report, is the inevitable sexual temptation arising from close proximity of men and women away from home and in stressful environments. An apparently naively title article 'Why do female troops get pregnant during deployment?' (*MedPageToday*, 6 September 2018) reported on the relatively high frequency of pregnancies in US military units on active service. It would not be too cynical to suggest that some of these pregnancies were not as unplanned as the article indicated, removing female combatants from harsh battle conditions such as in the Bosnia campaign. There is an ethical issue of placing in combat and danger women who may have recently become pregnant but may not have admitted to their superiors their true condition.

Sexual relationships might cause jealousy and perceived favouritism, and could have detrimental impact on the cohesion and effectiveness of the unit. This is not to blame female soldiers for male lust, but society has moved beyond the female eunuch and it is simply unrealistic in the twenty first century to think that such liaisons are anything but inevitable. Sexual interaction is the default when men and women in their prime are placed in close proximity, with little competition to what Field Marshal Montgomery described as 'horizontal refreshment'[202]. Surely it is obvious that mixing of the sexes will cause the very problems that the Wigston Report is so keen to eradicate?

---

202   Oulds R (2012): *Montgomery and the First War on Terror*. London: Bretwalda.

The social divide

The classless society, promoted by previous prime ministers John Major and Tony Blair, is a wishful-thinking fallacy. The enduring divide between the 'haves' and 'have-nots' has returned with a vengeance as people with power and privilege have reinforced their social status following the electoral shock of Brexit. A metropolitan elite that controls the political establishment and dominates the culture is disdainful if not contemptuous towards the 'great unwashed': the ordinary people who espouse faith, flag and family (McCrae, 16 June 2019):

This class divide is no news in the lower echelons of the armed services. Animosity of the ordinary soldiers to the officer class is never far from the surface, and erupts when those in authority show themselves to be out of touch with reality, as satirised in Richard Attenborough's musical *Oh What a Lovely War* and the television comedy *Black Adder*. 'Lions led by donkeys' is a phrase popularly used to contrast the brave men of the British infantry with the incompetent and callous generals who lead them, a theme illustrated by the First World War song *Hanging on the Old Barbed Wire*:–

> *If you want to find the Sergeant*
> *I know where he is, I know where he is, I know where he is.*
> *If you want to find the Sergeant, I know where he is,*
> *He's lying on the canteen floor.*
> *I've seen him, I've seen him, lying on the canteen floor,*
> *I've seen him, I've seen him, lying on the canteen floor.*
> *If you want to find the Quarter-bloke*
> *I know where he is, I know where he is, I know where he is.*
> *If you want to find the Quarter-bloke, I know where he is,*
> *He's miles and miles behind the line.*
> *I've seen him, I've seen him, miles and miles behind the line,*
> *I've seen him, I've seen him, miles and miles behind the line.*
> *If you want the Sergeant-major, I know where he is.*
> *I know where he is, I know where he is, I know where he is.*
> *He's tossing off the private's rum.*
> *I've seen him, I've seen him, tossing off the private's rum,*
> *I've seen him, I've seen him, tossing off the private's rum.*
> *If you want the CO, I know where he is.*
> *He's down in a deep dug-out.*
> *I've seen him, I've seen him, down in a deep dug-out,*

I've seen him, I've seen him, down in a deep dug-out.
If you want the old battalion,
I know where they are, I know where they are, I know where they are.
They're hanging on the old barbed wire.
I've seen 'em, I've seen 'em, hanging on the old barbed wire.
I've seen 'em, I've seen 'em, hanging on the old barbed wire.

Today, coaxed by politicians and bureaucrats in the Ministry of Defence, the officer class is imposing progressive-liberal ideology on the type of service that needs it least. Such thinking abhors patriotism, defies common sense, and is likely to be extremely destructive to Britain's famed fighting forces. Military effectiveness relies on an *espirit des corps*. Young men from working-class homes do not sign up to a sterile, corporate, unisex culture. They want to be with fellow lads, bonding as a 'band of brothers'. Their banter and rivalry are not 'inappropriate behaviours', but healthy outlets in a dangerous job.

Colonel Richard Kemp (*Daily Mail*, 14 January 2018) decried the Army being 'forced down a route of political correctness'. Yet 'political correctness' is a misnomer for actions that are neither political nor correct. It is a euphemism for subversion of traditional norms and beliefs, driven by identity politics and the underlying strategy of critical theory. The relentless progress of Marxist ideology has been achieved by disguising the wolf in sheep's clothing: politically correct ideals are presented as liberal, tolerant and inclusive, despite being the opposite. As cultural Marxism was described by Kurten & McCrae (19 September 2019), 'the serpent steals undetected through the undergrowth'. If people see this silently slithering snake, they stand back and do nothing, fearing its bite. Any naysayer risks being cast as intolerant or 'far right'.

Where a liberal moderniser sees change for the better, a conservative sees a last bastion falling to the 'march through the institutions'. The customary manpower of white working-class soldiers and middle-class officers is gradually changing in a multicultural and more female-orientated work environment, and inevitably a culture clash has arisen between the 'old school' and egalitarian idealists. It may seem that the latter are on the right side of history, yet there is room for optimism. Canadian psychologist and *guru* Jordan Peterson (2018) is an intellectual saviour of traditional male roles and responsibilities. Watching Peterson's videos, young men are beginning to realise that displaying 'wokeness' brings short-term social reward but ultimately curtails their life chances.

Meanwhile, 'woke' ideology is beginning to be derided by a small but growing number of free-thinking young men and women (though typically not from the guilt-ridden white middle class). They are bucking against the stifling censorship and witch hunts, as terrifying described by Greg Lukianoff and Jonathan Haidt in *The Coddling of the American Mind* (2018).

Summary

Curing the armed forces of 'wokeness' should be an immediate goal of Boris Johnson's administration. It is an acid test of competent conservatism. Of course there will be resistance from the Ministry of Defence, which welcomes the progressive diversion from the more pressing problem of determining the role of our armed forces in a world of threats ranging from a resurgent Russia to Islamic extremism. Tough decisions are deferred or avoided, in favour of easier gains in matters of dubious import such as diversifying regiments with women and transgender recruits. Perhaps after the political and military failure of the missions in Basra and Helmand provinces the 'top brass' are desperate to be liked, forgetting that first they need to be respected.

As shown in this response, the Inappropriate Behaviours report is a parody of political correctness, and likely to be counterproductive. Sexual abuse, bullying and racial discrimination must be tackled, but sociologist Robert K Merton's (1936) 'law of unintended consequences' should be heeded. For all Wigston's good intent, worse damage may be wreaked on individuals, teams, operational effectiveness and reputation by imposing a punitive 'woke' culture that stifles normal human behaviour in an often stressful and sometimes life-threatening environment. Leadership in our armed services should refocus on morale and military effectiveness. We should be deferential not to the virtue-signalling graduates pushing pens in Whitehall, but to the soldiers, sailors and airmen who put their lives on the line for us, Queen and country.

Glossary

Cultural Marxism – originated by the critical theorists of the Frankfurt School, who realised that a Bolshevik-style revolution was unlikely to succeed in democratic Western societies, this movement strives to overturn the underlying culture rather than adhering to the classic economic determinism of Karl Marx

Discrimination — literally to differentiate between one thing and another, but in more common usage meaning prejudicial behaviour towards categories of people

Identity politics — political alliances based on race, gender, sexual orientation or other group status, replacing traditionally broader party politics

Inappropriate behaviours – behaviours deemed inappropriate

LGBT – lesbian, gay, bisexual and transgender

Mansplaining — a man talking to a woman in a condescending manner, or controlling a conversation to suppress women's participation

Micro-aggressions — everyday verbal or behavioural slights, typically unintentional, conveying prejudicial ideas about a category of person or group

Patriarchy — a social system or culture in which men are dominant over women

Political correctness – a strategy to deter or banish words or behaviour that exclude, marginalise or disparage groups of people perceived as socially disadvantaged

Racism – racial discrimination, or behaviour perceived as racist

Sexism — sexual discrimination, or behaviour perceived as sexist

Stereotype — a culturally prevalent but simplistic idea about a particular type of person or people (e.g. Germans have no sense of humour)

Unconscious bias – beliefs based on stereotypes that are likely to cause prejudicial behaviour

White privilege – the idea that white people (particularly male) were born with a silver spoon in their mouths, and will not relinquish their advantaged status

Woke — heightened concern with injustice in society (initially self-ascribed, this term is now more commonly used for ridicule)

References

American Psychological Association (2019): *APA Issues First Ever Guidelines for Practice with Men and Boys.* https://www.apa.org/about/policy/boys-men-practice-guidelines.pdf

Collins T (10 July 2016): How the army must reshape after Chilcot. *Daily Telegraph.* https://www.telegraph.co.uk/men/thinking-man/how-the-army-must-reshape-after-chilcot/

Daily Mail (14 January 2018): Prayer time on patrol: British Army defies critics of politically correct campaign as it releases new recruitment video showing Muslim soldier praying in front of his colleagues. *https://www.dailymail.co.uk/news/article-5267601/Army-advert-shows-Muslim-soldier-praying.html*

Daily Mail (27 September 2018): 'I wouldn't change anything we did on the night': Grenfell families' fury after London's fire chief defends 'stay put' policy as fire raged. *https://www.dailymail.co.uk/news/article-6214657/London-fire-chief-believe-seeing-Grenfell.html*

Daily Telegraph (24 February 2009): Institutional racism: a decade of self-flagellation (editorial). https://www.telegraph.co.uk/comment/telegraph-view/4800954/Institutional-racism-a-decade-of-self-flagellation.html

Kemp R (5 April 2016): Putting women on the front line is dangerous PC meddling. We will pay for it in blood. *Daily Telegraph.* https://www.telegraph.co.uk/news/2016/04/05/putting-women-on-the-front-line-is-dangerous-pc-meddling-we-will/

Kurten D, McCrae N (19 September 2019): The problem with cultural Marxism. *European Conservative.* https://europeanconservative.com/2019/09/the-problem-with-cultural-marxism/

Lukianoff G, Haidt J (2018): *The Coddling of the American Mind: How Good Intentions and Bad Ideas are Setting Up a Generation for Failure.* Allen Lane.

McCrae N (16 June 2019): The divided sate of Britain. *Human Events.* https://humanevents.com/2019/06/16/the-divided-state-we-are-in/

MedPageToday (6 September 2018): Why do female troops get pregnant during deployment? https://www.medpagetoday.com/publichealthpolicy/militarymedicine/74959

Merton RK (1936): The unanticipated consequences of purposive social action. *American Sociological Review,* 1: 894-904.

Ministry of Defence (2019): *Report on Inappropriate Behaviours.* https://www.gov.uk/government/publications/wigston-review-into-inappropriate-behaviours

Murray D (2019): *The Madness of Crowds: Gender, Race and Identity.* London: Bloomsbury Continuum.

Novak KJ, Brown RA, Frank J (2011): Women on patrol: an analysis of differences in officer arrest behaviour. *Policing: an International Journal of Police Strategies and Management,* 34:566-587

Peterson J (2018): *12 Rules for Life: an Antidote to Chaos.* Allen Lane.

Pinker S (2002): *The Blank Slate: the Modern Denial of Human Nature.* Allen Lane.

Times (2 April 2018): Metropolitan Police ditches practice of believing all victims. https://www.thetimes.co.uk/article/police-ditch-practice-of-believing-all-victims-jsg6qd2ws#

Vice News (14 September 2017): Gay people make more money than their straight peers. https://www.vice.com/en_us/article/59dm4q/gay-people-make-more-money-than-their-straight-peers

Volkman E (1995): *Espionage: the Greatest Spy Operations of the 20th Century.* New York: John Wiley & Sons.

World Economic Forum (8 October 2018): Women are more productive than men, according to new research. https://www.weforum.org/agenda/2018/10/women-are-more-productive-than-men-at-work-these-days

Index

Abortion 68
Adorno, Theodor 15
Aitken, Robin 63
Alcoholics Anonymous 75
Allen, Woody 15
Always (tampons) 66-67
American Psychological
   Association 86
Anhedonia 41
Armed services 82-94
Asch, Solomon 38
Asylum-seekers 67
Attenborough, Richard 92
Authoritarianism 12-13

Baddeley, Michelle 41
Bandura, Albert 37
Barnabas Fund 72
Barnett, Ronald 54
Beech, Carl 84
Benoit, Sophia 64
Black Adder 92
Black History Month 44
Blair, Tony 11, 28, 43, 70, 92
Boghossian, Peter 74
Bolsheviks 15
Bonaparte, Napoleon 60
Brand, Jo 63
Brexit 8, 21, 24-25, 30, 42, 46-49,
   62, 63, 67, 69, 72-73, 92
British Broadcasting Corporation
   (BBC) 12, 46, 63-64
Broadbent, Ben 29
Brown, Gordon 70
Burkeman, Oliver 31

Cable Street, Battle of 76
Cambridge Spy Ring 87
Canning Town 76
Canterbury 22
Capitalism 19
Cavilla-Sforza, Luca 37
Censorship 32-34
Chakrabarti, Lady 58
Channel Four 73
Cherry, Joanna 42
China 13, 20, 34, 50
Chomsky, Noam 40
Christian / Judeo-Christian
   culture 15, 26, 49
Christian, Terry 47
Churchill, Winston 49
Civil Service 61, 75, 76
Climate change 50-51, 61-62, 76
Clinton, Hillary 24
College of Policing 33-34
Collins, Tim 89-90
Comedy / comedians 41, 63, 72-74
Communism 13, 14, 44, 52, 77
Conservative Party 22-23, 25, 27, 69
Cotton, Dany 88
Criado Perez, Carole 23
Cromwell, Thomas 69
Crown Prosecution Service 33
Cultural appropriation 38, 66
Cultural Marxism 14-17, 39, 44,
   58, 93
Cummings, Dominic 75

Daily Express 64
Daily Mail 42, 64

Daily Telegraph 27, 64
Dale, Iain 42
Darwin, Charles 37
Daubney, Martin 55
Davos 61
Dawes, Emily 55
Dawkins, Richard 37, 47
Decolonisation 44, 54
Delingpole, James 50-51
Democratic Party 24
Derrida, Jacques 17
Dick, Cressida 88
Dickens, Charles 44
Duchess of Sussex (Meghan Markle) 39, 58
Dutschke, Rudi 16

Eatwell, Roger 24
Equality Act 2010 70-71
Equity (actors' union) 59
Ersson, Elin 70
European Convention of Human Rights 33-34, 69
European Court of Human Rights 32
European Union (EU) 8, 26, 29, 47-48, 50, 51, 60, 68
Evening Standard 64
Evolution theory 37-38
Extinction Rebellion 76
Eysenck, Hans 12

Falangismo movement 13
Family 19, 26
Farage, Nigel 22
Fascism 13
Faye, Jean-Pierre 13
Feldman, Marcus 37

Feminism 18, 23, 42, 52-53, 63, 65-66, 69
Foucault, Michel 17
Fox, Laurence 58
Franco, Francisco 13
Frank, Tom 24
Frankfurt School 15, 51
Freedom of speech 32-34, 40-41, 53-55, 68-69
Free Speech Union 68-69
Fukuyama, Francis 35

Gervais, Rickie 65
Ghandi, Mahatma 78
Gilets jaunes 27
Gillette 65-66
Glastonbury Festival 46
Globalism 26, 61-62
Goldberg, Jonah 77
Golden Globes 65
Goodhart, David 22
Goodwin, Matthew 24
Gordon, Bryony 75
Gove, Michael 25
Gramsci, Antonio 7, 15-16
Gray, John 8, 78
Greer, Bonnie 59
Grenfell Tower 88
Guardian 27, 46, 59, 64

Haidt, Jonathan 14, 57, 94
Hale, Lady 42
Hallam, Roger 76
Hanging on the Old Barbed Wire 92
Hate speech / crime 32-34, 40, 70-72
Hazony, Yoram 60
Heath, Ted 27
Heffer, Simon 50

Help for Heroes 82
Henry VIII, King 69
Hive (software company) 87-88
Hollywood 64-65, 66
Horkheimer, Max 15
Horseshoe 13
Humberside Police 33
Humphreys, John 63
Hungary 26

Immigration 26, 27-34, 61-62
Identity politics 17-19, 23, 35, 42, 45-46, 52, 55, 57, 66, 74, 76
Information technology companies 45-46
Intersectionality 18
Islam 31-32, 38
Islamophobia 40, 71

Jacobs, Sherelle 78
James, Oliver 19
Jihad 35, 41, 65
Johnson, Boris 8, 25, 42, 49, 53, 75, 94
Jong-Il, Kim 65
Judaism 15
Juvenal 46

Kaufmann, Eric 32, 50
Kemp, Richard 90-91, 93
King, Martin Luther 59
King's College London 48
Kumar, Nish 73
Kurten, David 93

Labour Party 11, 21-25, 28-31, 43, 67, 68, 70, 76
Lacan, Jacques 17

Lammy, David 47
Lasch, Christopher 41
Lawrence, Stephen 84
Le Corbusier, Charles-Édouard 27
Leafe, Richard 35
Lenin, Vladimir 7
Liberal Democrat Party 62
Liddle, Rod 24
Lindsay, James 74
London Fire Brigade 88
Long-Bailey, Rebecca 49, 68
Lukianoff, Greg 57, 94

MacPherson Report 84
Mahmood, Khalid 71
Major, John 92
Mandelson, Peter 28
Manning, Bernard 73
Mansfield 23
Marcuse, Herbert 15-16
Marketing 18-19, 39
Marx, Karl 13, 14
Masculinity 8, 25, 65-66, 83, 86-87
Mason, Paul 30
May, Theresa 12, 62
McEwan, Ian 47
McGrath, Titania 74
McGowan, Rose 65
Mehmet, Alp 31
Mein Kampf 74
Memes 37-38
Mental health 57
Merkel, Angela 26
Mermaids (charity) 53
Merton, Robert K 94
MeToo movement 41, 65, 84-85
Metro (newspaper) 64
Metropolitan Police 84, 88

Middle class 18, 19, 35, 41, 46-47
Midwifery 53
Migration Watch 31
Mill, John Stuart 60
Miller, Alistair 32
Miller, Gina 42
Miller, Harry 33-34
Ministry of Defence 82, 93, 94
Mirza, Munira 53
Mishra, Pankaj 49
Mohammed, Prophet 32, 38
Möller, Thomas 32
Money-Coutts, Sophia 64
Montgomery, Bernard 91
Morrissey, Steven Patrick 30
Murray, Douglas 77, 86-87
Muslim Council for Britain 53, 71
Muslims 26, 29-30, 35, 71, 72, 83

National Front 28
National Health Service (NHS)
    28-29, 60
National identity 8, 48-49, 54,
    60-62, 67
Nazi Germany 13, 15, 60
Netflix 64
New Culture Forum 49
Newham 29
Newspapers 64
Non-playing character (NPC) 73-74
Norcott, Geoff 72
Nuremberg trials 76

Obama, Barack 56
Oh What a Lovely War 92-93
Oliver, Jamie 66
Open Society Foundation 17
Orwell, George 13, 17, 40

Osborne, George 64

Patriarchy 18, 35, 44, 86
People's Party 24
Perkins, Adam 12
Peterson, Jordan 57, 93
Phillips, Jess 35
Phillips, Trevor 18, 43
Pink News 74
Pinker, Steven 86
Pluckrose, Helen 74
Poitier, Sidney 28
Poland 26
Police Scotland 72
Policy Exchange 55, 71
Population growth 31
Populism 22, 24
Portes, Jonathan 48
Portland State University 74
Poujadistes 23
Powell, Enoch 27-28
Pride (gay festival) 66
Proms (Royal Albert Hall) 50

Question Time 58, 63

Racism 30-31, 42, 46-48, 54,
    56-57, 58-60, 73, 84
Radio 4 63
Readers Digest 74
Red magazine 42
Red pills 56
Reich, Wilhelm 15, 25-26
Rhodes, Cecil 44
Rochester 30
Roman Catholicism 7, 68
Routledge, Clay 66
Rowbotham, S 18

Rowling, JK 41-42
Rutherford, Jonathan 34
Sainsbury, Lord 60-61
Sartre, Jean-Paul 41
Schools 43-44, 53
Schwab, Klaus 61-62
Scottish National Party 48
Seacole, Mary 44
Secularism 19
Segal, L 18
Shakespeare, William 44
Sheffield, University of 56-57
Sibelius, Jean 50
Silicon Valley 45-46
Sinn Fein 48
Smith, Adam 61
Smith, Angela 31
Social learning theory 37
Social media 10, 40, 41, 45-46
Socialism 13, 16, 26, 51
Soleimani, Qassem 65
Soros, George 17
Soubry, Anna 47
Southampton, University of 55
Soviet Union 15, 20, 25-26, 34, 60, 77
Stasi 20
Stock, Kathleen 71
Stonewall 71
Stormzy 78
Student unions 55
Surveillance 69-71, 76
Sweden 32, 70, 77
Swinson, Jo 62

Team America – World Police 65
Tell Mama 71
Thatcher, Margaret 67, 88

Thornberry, Emily 30
Thunberg, Greta 8, 51, 78
Thwaites, Sir Bryan 43
Toynbee, Polly 29
Trade unions 67-68
Transgenderism 7, 25, 33-34, 35, 41, 52-53, 66-67, 71, 74, 77
Trotsky, Leon 8, 51
Trump, Donald 25, 52, 59-60, 61, 64, 65, 74
Turkish Airlines 70
Twitter 33, 46, 59, 63, 65, 74

Unison (trade union) 67
United States Marine Corps 89
Universities 43-44, 53-55, 56-57, 58
Urban, Mark 61

Virtue signalling 19-21, 35, 43, 69

Wainwright H 18
Waitrose 47
Ward, Julie 69
Watt, Nick 11
Weinstein, Harvey 65
Welsh, Tom 76
West, Kanye 60
White working class 18, 29, 30, 43-44
Whittle, Peter 49
Wigston, Michael 82
Wigston Report 82-94
Williams, Rowan 18
Wolverhampton 27
Women's Equality Party 23
Workers of England (trade union) 68
World Economic Forum 61-62
World Trade Center 35

Yes Minister 61
Young, Toby 68
Young Vic Theatre 20
YouTube 73

Zedong, Mao 8
Zuckerberg, Mark 46

CPSIA information can be obtained
at www.ICGtesting.com
Printed in the USA
LVHW101540120820
662977LV00020BA/2536